D0812032

why jobs die
&
what to do about it

ROBERT N. FORD

why jobs die
&
what to do about it

job redesign
&
future productivity

SALVE REGINA UNIVERSITY
LIBRARY
NEWPORT, RI 02840-4192

amacom

A DIVISION OF AMERICAN MANAGEMENT ASSOCIATIONS

For Jane,
Rennie, and Rayme

This book was set in Century Expanded and Helvetica Bold by
The Fuller Organization, Inc.
It was designed by Beata Gray.
Printer and binder were The Alpine Press, Inc.

Library of Congress Cataloging in Publication Data

Ford, Robert N
  Why jobs die & what to do about it.

  Bibliography: p.
  Includes index.
  1. Job enrichment.   2. Work design.
3. Motivation (Psychology)   I. Title.
HF5549.5.J616F67   658.31'42   79-11307
ISBN 0-8144-5502-6

© 1979 AMACOM
A division of American Management Associations, New York. All rights reserved.
Printed in the United States of America.

This publication may not be reproduced, stored in a retrieval system, or
transmitted in whole or in part, in any form or by any means, electronic,
mechanical, photocopying, recording, or otherwise, without the prior written
permission of AMACOM, 135 West 50th Street, New York, N.Y. 10020.

First Printing

I have not brought misery upon my fellows.
I have not made the beginning of every day
laborious in the sight of him who worked for me.

From the ancient Egyptian *Book of the Dead,*
"Confession of the Righteous Soul"

foreword

IN THE LATE 1960s I was spending most of my professional time as an industrial engineer working on productivity problems on the European continent. The writing was on the wall; to an experienced observer, it was clear that rank-and-file workers, whether in the shop or in offices, would not accept for much longer the usual industrial engineering and cost improvement techniques for job improvement any more than workers in the United States. It was either outright rejection, as in Italy, or passive resistance, as in France and the Low Countries. This is another way of saying that worker alienation was threatening to bring to a standstill the perennial drive for higher productivity.

Knowing that new management concepts are normally "made in U.S.A.," I started the search for practical solutions back home. I was appalled to find that despite the breakthrough of Frederick Herzberg, many, if not most, psychologists and industrial engineers were in strong disagreement and were actually engaged in verbal polemics.

The result? For most industrial engineers and scores of management people, the behavioral science approach to job development was just a lot of theoretical talk "to make employees happy." It would cost money, they said. By the same token, many psychologists were saying that "Taylorism" had run its course and that industrial engineering, which historically had been the source of job fragmentation and monotony, was on its way out. Neither side was right, of course, but controversy slowed down the practical application of behavioral science to productivity increase.

In 1972, through a recommendation of John R. Maher of IBM, I had the good fortune to be introduced to Bob Ford and to work with him in several countries. Bob is a hands-on practitioner. Herzberg and his predecessors, too numerous to mention, have brought us theories of motivation and the basic principles of "what makes a person really tick on his job." Bob picked up from there, and quickly became recognized as *the* job design and motivation practitioner who got things done. In fact, he became the undisputed leader in the art of implementing these new behavioral science principles, whether in shops, in offices, or on service activities. His successes at AT&T and in the Bell System are now classics that speak for themselves.

At that time, precious few industrial engineers and psychologists had grasped the concept that for best results in cost improvement, the Herzberg behavioral science findings had to be wedded to industrial engineering techniques. Likewise, we industrial engineers (and systems people, too) had not yet realized that we had to change our own time-honored behavior patterns. The days of the "one best way," to be developed by the omnipotent industrial engineer (Bob calls him "super guru"), were over. Most important, industrial engineers had to make a 180-degree turn and use their skills, in methods and work measurement, to make jobs richer and more meaningful instead of fragmenting them. Only then would they be able to assist top management to change the attitudes of middle management and supervision. I started promoting this idea in the early seventies, and was met by stony silence, to say the least.

Two statements Bob Ford made to me stuck with me. He was the first social psychologist I had met who thoroughly endorsed the campaign I had started. He told me that a bridge between behavior scientists and industrial engineers had to be built, for the benefit of both professions and business at large. When I asked him who in an organization should implement the principles he was promoting in his first book (*Motivation Through the Work Itself*), he replied, "It can be done by personnel people or the industrial engineers. I prefer the industrial engineers, because the construction of jobs is a part of their profession, and they are trained to get action."

What Bob and I are preaching—he the social psychologist and I the career industrial engineer—is that these two disciplines are not antagonistic but complementary. Industrial engineers, especially the old-timers steeped in tradition, will have to change their behavior. Only then can they help develop positive attitudes among supervisors and ultimately among the rank and file. Once they grasp this, they can become the industrial engineers that the future will demand.

The following might serve as an illustration of the need for cooperation between these two disciplines. Many of us have perhaps forgotten that the First Lady of Industrial Engineering, Dr. Lillian Gilbreth, was a doctor of psychology. She had wed industrial engineer Frank B. Gilbreth. Has this marriage facilitated the development of the many industrial engineering innovations the Gilbreths have brought to our profession?

In his second book, Bob Ford underscores why and how

the lack of understanding and cooperation between engineers and management on one side and behavioral science practitioners on the other leads to the creation of "dumb-dumb jobs." Chapter 2, "Why Jobs Die," in which he writes about "perfect practices," departmentalization of responsibility, wrong measurement plans, and the like, includes some truly illuminating examples of such jobs. One of the most dramatic and impressive statements in the book is made by a Canadian colleague of Ford's. They were talking about the high rates of force loss, but he was more concerned with "the great number of people we've lost who are still with us,"—the many people who, for any number of reasons, stay in jobs that they no longer find fulfilling.

All this said—and brought forward in this book—it is indeed frightening that, with the exception of postgraduate training, there are still no college-level industrial engineering courses that teach embryo engineers how to change traditional attitudes and work habits and how to use proven concepts of motivation in combination with traditional engineering concepts. By comparison, Sweden, which is way ahead of us in job redesign and the application of priniciples of motivation, has willingly negotiated the "marriage" of the two disciplines. In 1972 the Swedish Employers' and Trade Union Federations reached a most interesting "Agreement on Rationalization." Among other things, it specified that "the industrial engineers and outside experts [that is, the consultants] ought to have satisfactory training in such matters as methods analysis and measurement—and also industrial psychology." Unfortunately this agreement has remained a dead letter because of the lack of engineers with appropriate backgrounds, but this does not alter the fact that Swedish business recognized in 1972 a need which American business has not formally recognized. In fact, in Sweden both parties have formed an Industrial Engineering Training Committee, one objective of which is to influence the training of industrial engineers in the desired direction. When will American educational and business communities wake up to that need?

One of the most important points put forth in the book is the need for *participation* at all levels. When we finally reach the point where supervisors and subordinates participate in redesigning jobs or, better still, initiate the effort, we will have won most of the battle. Many people are aware of the amazing success that Japan has had in increasing its productivity to rates two to three times those of the United States and those of its European competitors, but many are not aware of the part played by the principles of participation, particularly decision making at all levels, from the workshop to the company president's office. These principles are rooted in Japan's history and are an integral part of its present organizational concepts.

If we fail to learn from Japan's experience and further ignore the concepts this book espouses, there will be no obstacles left to Japan's drive to become the No. 1 industrial nation in the free world.

SERGE A. BIRN
Consulting Management Engineer
Louisville, Kentucky

preface

THE AUTOMOBILE INDUSTRY is plagued with absenteeism on Mondays, Fridays, and the days just before or after a holiday. Perhaps 15 to 25 percent of the workforce may be absent, wreaking havoc on production schedules. At one time, in an effort to combat the disease, Chrysler Corporation went so far as to offer green stamps as a bonus to those who appeared for work on the problem days. General Motors has tried giving away sets of monogrammed drinking glasses. But, as one spokesman said in 1972, "We don't have the answers. One thing is sure: If they won't come in for $30.50 a day, they won't come in for a monogrammed glass."* Since then, the average wage has probably doubled.

Why not just give up Mondays as a bad idea and work only four days? This, in fact, is a growing trend, especially in small or new industries. Four days of ten hours each rather than five days of eight hours each. But the hope that the signs of low motivation such as absenteeism will disappear may be wishful thinking.

*J. Gooding, *The Job Revolution,* New York: Walker, 1972, p. 112.

Such a tactic accepts the problem and tries to live with it. *The New York Times* reports this experience with the four-day workweek:

> Gordon S. Carbonneau, the president of Carbonneau Industries, a loudspeaker manufacturer in Grand Rapids, Michigan, made the change in 1953, but two years later his 250 workers voted to go back to five days.
>
> Although the hours were juggled, the work was still dull, he said. Once the novelty wore off, he recalled, the women felt under greater pressure to produce the same number of loudspeakers in four days even though they had the same number of hours.
>
> "There's an element of gimmickry in this," he added. "Soldering loudspeakers is pretty monotonous. Just changing the work day doesn't make the work more meaningful."*

In my personal experience, management has worked long and hard at stemming the downward slide of jobs, principally through improving maintenance factors—that is, changing aspects that surround the job rather than changing the monotonous job itself. Such changes don't seem to work, not for long. No amount of moralizing or reasoning with employees ("All we ask is an honest day's work for an honest day's pay") has any appreciable effect. We've got to stop and look at the work itself.

Many people are thinking and writing in this field now. My first book, *Motivation Through the Work Itself,* reported on 19 field experiments in the Bell System.† I own 26 other books on the subject of jobs published since then.

The fad stage for job enrichment is over now. In the early 1970s all three major TV networks in the United States carried programs about job enrichment. Entire conferences were organized around the theme. This trend too

---

The New York Times, March 20, 1971.
† R. N. Ford, *Motivation Through the Work Itself,* New York: AMACOM, 1969.

seems to be dying down, perhaps for the better, as perennial conference-goers turn to newer "solutions."

We in this field are now talking about the problem recently called job enrichment as job design and work organization. The words "work" and "job" are not synonymous here: A "job" is a slice of some "work" that needs to be done. Two problems may occur: (1) The work may not need to be done, or (2) the work may have been sliced into poor jobs, nonmotivating jobs. Job enrichment is now viewed as only one solution to the bigger problem of work flow, job design, and work organization.

This book concentrates on the job slices that motivate. It assumes, generally, that there is work that needs to be done. Astute managers who follow the development here will know that they must answer this question first: Why do this work at all? Even if the work as a whole needs to be done, managers will learn that the failure to design good jobs will often result in duplication of the work, in personnel assigned to "checking," "coordinating," and "expediting"—steps that might be avoided under other job and work designs.

Part 1 of this book tells managers:
— What causes jobs to go sour.
— How to recognize jobs that are unnecessarily bad.
— How to redesign the job itself, and how to design jobs well in the first place when there is a new work flow.
— How to set up and organize a group of jobs so that they make sense together in case a particular job defies improvement.
Part II is quite different. The two chapters permit managers (or employees) to analyze the quality of their own job, to rate it from excellent to poor. And if their job is unsatisfactory, Part II offers some strategies for improving it.

Along the way, the issue of ethics will be raised. Are the proposals for job design and work organization ethical? Is this merely another fad, another clever way of manipulating helpless employees?

Job design and work organization people are not mad at the four-day week, longer vacations, flexible working hours, paid dental care, paid legal care, job security programs, and similar benefits that workers are struggling for. The job design and work organization person may suspect that these are "cop-outs," ways of avoiding dealing directly with the unnecessarily bad jobs—a bribe: "Please do this stupid work and I'll give you a big bag of jelly beans." Adequate maintenance factors are necessary, but they're not a substitute for good, meaningful jobs. All that and jelly beans too; that is the credo of the job design and work organization person.

We need to concern ourselves with how well or poorly we use employees for a reason that did not exist ten years ago. Since 1973, the OPEC countries have quadrupled the price of oil. For the forseeable future this will be an uncontrollable cost; we must have oil or some form of energy, and we must pay for it. The pressure is on, as never before, to get the most out of our employees. More and more automation by machinery that demands more and more energy is not the panacea it once seemed. Therefore, in addition to paying people well, in addition to treating them well, we must use them well. This book aims to help managers utilize people well, not only to the satisfaction of the organization, but to that of the individual.

I have written about bad jobs and what to do about them just as though I thought up all these ideas myself. I didn't, of course, but I want to keep my story uncluttered. If I gave everyone credit, the list would run to a hundred names. Should you recognize an idea that you think is yours, be consoled by the dictum I follow in my writing, "Never steal trash."

ROBERT N. FORD
Punta Gorda, Florida
January 1979

contents

part I

---

job design and
work organization

1

the problem

THERE ARE GOOD REASONS why a manager should pay attention to the young movement of job design and work organization. It not only promises economies in the immediate future but also offers long-term economies to the organization, or any part of it, in its struggle to survive. In addition employees will like the kind of job designs and organizations that emerge from application of the concepts in this book.

Let me state the general case for embarking on a course of job design and work organization:

1. There is a problem in the industrialized world.
2. Jobs vary widely in quality; some are very unrewarding.
3. The attitude of employees toward their work is certainly not improving.
4. New evidence suggests that job satisfaction may greatly affect life expectancy.
5. Virtually no organization is exempt from the risk of "job death"; this holds for all jobs, including management jobs.
6. It takes time to get results; start now.
7. Some jobs may be dying now, without startling symptoms as yet.

A Problem

We are constantly being reminded that there is "a problem" in the land. Employees don't want to work. They overtly sabotage the thing they work on, the very source of their livelihood. They deliberately restrict productivity. They resist management's attempts to produce more goods at a lower unit cost when any rational observer will tell you that this is the road toward economic abundance. Simply put, the problem is this: People just don't want to work these days. This is the era of the "goof-off" employee, of the careless, poor-quality effort. My travels have taught me that this point of view is held not only in the United States but in all Western industrialized nations; for example, in most of Western Europe, in Scandinavia, Canada, South Africa, and Japan.

You may agree or disagree with this often-stated, "cocktail-party-ish" description of workers. I tend to disagree, although I have known a few employees who were perennial goof-offs. Either way, a problem does exist: A national resource—the talent of our people—is being wasted. Our people have the ability to be more productive, better meet customer/client needs, make our organizations run more smoothly, and make their own lives more fulfilling.

In modern, industrialized societies, the pressure to make better jobs will vary from year to year as economic conditions fluctuate. The job design effort experienced a setback in 1974-75 with the economic downturn. But the pressure returns with each upturn in the business cycle. When jobs are more plentiful, when employees are not chained to their posts by the "golden handcuffs," they wander off in search of jobs that pay as well, or perhaps better, but that meet their ideas of what a good job should be.

America must *use* its people well, not merely *treat* them well with high salaries and fringe benefits. Economic life for America is not as simple as it was in the pre-OPEC days, before the Arabic nations controlled the price of oil. At this writing the balance of international payments is persistently running against the United States. There is no letup in pressure from such competitive economies as those of Japan, Taiwan, and the many industrialized nations of Western Europe. Manufacturers in these countries are making life difficult in such areas as automobiles, electronics, optics, textiles, wood, shipbuilding, and steel. Our acknowledged world leadership in aviation is suddenly threatened by the European consortium Airbus Industrie, and our leadership in automobile tires, by Michelin.

This is a vastly complicated international economic mess. Clearly, there is no one answer. But one thing is certain: America cannot afford to waste its most valuable resource—its people.

Variation in Job Quality

We simply must put off the person who says all work is bad, or all work is good. To my knowledge, the most persuasive statistics ever published on variation in job quality were compiled in 1972 by Robert L. Kahn of the Survey Research Center at the University of Michigan. The statistics, in Table 1, come from the responses of 3,000 workers in several studies to a group of questions related to the following major question: Would you choose similar work again, if you had it to do over? After properly cautioning us to the fact that not all the basic studies used precisely the same procedures, and that the table omits hundreds of jobs, Kahn concludes, "The table is remarkable for the range of response—from 93 percent of university professors to 16 percent of unskilled auto workers say they would seek the same type of work again."

Monetary reward does not completely explain the differences in attitudes of these people toward their jobs. I would hazard a guess that the auto workers (skilled and

Table 1. Percentages of people who would choose similar work again, by occupational group.

Professional and White-Collar Occupations	Percent	Skilled Trades and Blue-Collar Occupations	Percent
Urban university professors	93	Skilled printers	52
Mathematicians	91	Paper workers	42
Physicists	89	Skilled auto workers	41
Biologists	89	Skilled steelworkers	41
Chemists	86	Textile workers	31
Firm lawyers	85	Blue-collar workers	24
School superintendents	85	Unskilled steelworkers	21
Lawyers	83	Unskilled auto workers	16
Journalists (Washington correspondents)	82		
Church university professors	77		
Solo lawyers	75		
White-collar workers (nonprofessional)	43		

Source: Robert L. Kahn, "Worker Alienation, 1972," testimony to the U.S. Senate, Committee on Labor and Public Welfare, U.S. Senate, 92nd Congress, S3916, July 25–26, 1972, pp. 268-269; reprinted in "The Work Module: A Proposal for the Humanization of Work," *Work and the Quality of Life,* James O'Toole, ed., Cambridge, Mass.: MIT Press, 1974.

unskilled) earn more money than do the church university professors. Yet 77 percent of these professors said they would choose similar work again, while only 41 percent of skilled and 16 percent of unskilled auto workers said that they would.

Perhaps it goes without saying that attitudes toward any job vary widely—and that there is significant variation in job aspects within any one job classification. From my own knowledge of switchboard operators at five different kinds of switchboards in the telephone industry, there were striking differences in the way the operators rated their jobs, despite a uniform pay scale. People with a knowledge of job design and work organization could predict which kind of operating job was most highly prized; it was attending the long-distance switchboards. Although there is a relation between pay and willingness to choose a similar occupation again, the correlation is far from perfect. White-collar workers may be the most poorly paid of the occupation groups listed in Table 1, yet 43 percent would choose their work again. Urban college professors are not the most highly paid, yet almost all would choose their occupation again. Choosing or refusing jobs is more complicated than pay, even when the pay is seductively high. A foreman I was interviewing said, "After a few years as a foreman I got so fed up with paper work at night, with the heartaches going along with trying to do a good job by the company and by your men too, that I just decided to ask for my tools back again. I wanted to go back on my truck again, where I was boss of myself, at least, once I left the garage in the morning. This job redesign thing wiped out a major heartache, that unnecessary paper work." A young woman who accepted the responsibility of compiling entire telephone directories for several small cities remarked in an interview, "When I got out my first directory all by myself I—well—I just floated." Her clerical-level job was well below that of the foreman, but the work was rewarding to her. Jobs at any level in an organization can be rewarding psychologically. At least they should be. The middle manager man on rotation to company headquarters who remarked, "My problem is that I have no immediate problem," is a sad case. And a pay raise won't help the situation, not in the long run.

Attitudes Toward Jobs Deteriorating

The oldest continuing report on what employees think of their jobs that I know of is issued by Opinion Research Corp. of Princeton, New Jersey. It covers 159 companies and dates back to the early 1950s. A recent Associated

Press release on that report (August 10, 1977) pointed out that the percentage of clerical workers who are unhappy with their work has risen since 1952 from 24 percent to 32 percent. Among hourly workers, the percentage is up from 31 percent to 38 percent. Incidentally, for the same time period the percentage in each group who rated their pay unsatisfactory has dropped.

So, the issue isn't pay. And worker participation in management isn't the answer either. In a statement to United Press International on August 5, 1977, Jerome M. Rosow, president of the Work in America Institute, said: "Co-determination in the boardroom is of no interest to labor or management." A number of other officials from both labor and managment are quoted similarly in the U.P.I. release.

Knowledgeable people are making surprising bets on possible results of the mounting job dissatisfaction. A U.P.I. story of October 30, 1977, quotes James E. Durbin, president of Marriott Hotels Division, as follows:

> Durbin said he envisaged "considerable continued growth of tourism in the next quarter of the century. As job functions become more programmed with more people finding the novelty and challenge missing in their work-a-day lives, people will turn in increasing numbers to travel and leisure-time activities to escape boredom. This augurs well for the tourist industry."

I wish the tourist industry well, of course, but it does occur to me, as I watch customers being treated rudely as they travel, that hotel, motel, and fast-food businesses are not exempt from the very problem that Durbin says leads people to tourism.

At least three factors must be considered in accounting for the growing job dissatisfaction:

1. Jobs tend to die. That observation led me to write this book. I trust that the case presented here will be persuasive, for this need not happen.

2. New jobs are frequently less demanding intellectually than are their predecessors. In *Work is Here to Stay, Alas,* Sar A. Levitan and W. B. Johnston, two of America's foremost manpower specialists, say, "Millions of dull factory jobs remain, and millions of equally dull office jobs have been lately added to the job market."*

3. The expectation of young people as to the quality of jobs they will get is directly tied to their level of education. And their level of education is rising at the very time that the quality of jobs is deteriorating. This important gap is the basis for alienation from work.

The upper curve in Figure 1 shows the educational fix we are in. By 1976, 84 percent of Americans age 20 through 24 could produce at least a high school diploma. This figure has doubled since the start of World War II, an amazing fact about the United States. The figure is for men and women combined, because there is no important difference in educational level of young men and women after 1960. The growth rate is slowing down, as it must when it approaches 100 percent. But estimates indicate that perhaps 90 percent of young people will be high school graduates by 1990.*

The steepness of the educational rise for blacks is even more pronounced than for whites. Particularly striking is the fourfold increase in the enrollment of black females in colleges between the years 1966 and 1976. By 1976, 33 percent of high school graduates ages 20 to 24 were enrolled in colleges, a proportion that is holding fairly steady, even though the proportion finishing high school is still rising a bit. All will not finish college, but about 50 percent of these young people can now lay claim not only to a high school diploma but to at least one year beyond that. Our population has changed, and most other industrialized countries show the same changes.

*Salt Lake City: Olympus, 1973, p. 109.
*D.F. Johnson, "Education of Workers: Projections to 1990," *Monthly Labor Review,* November 1973, p. 25.

The lower curve in Figure 1 is hypothetical. It represents what Levitan, Johnston, Durbin, and I are talking about. It says: Suppose a given job appealed reasonably well to many high school graduates. Let's pick 44 percent, to give us a common point of departure, and assume these graduates would be willing to take the job and keep it for a reasonable period of time. By 1970, not as many would rate that job as highly. The falling curve illustrates this.

Figure I. The growing mismatch for a given job.

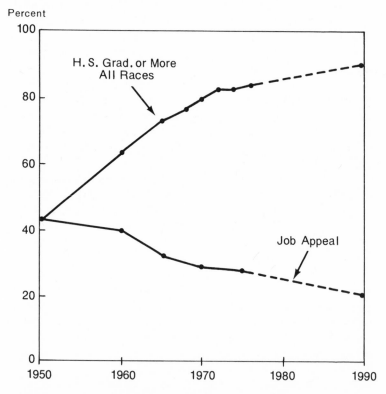

SOURCE: U.S. Bureau of the Census, "Characteristics of American Children and Youth: 1976," *Current Population Reports*, Series P-23, No. 66, Washington, D.C.: U.S. Government Printing Office, 1978.

Why does this happen? Either the job would be dying, or job changes (such as partial automation) would have eroded the job, or the current employee would still be holding the job only because he or she could find no job more suitable to his or her educational accomplishment. It's either work or starve, if not food-wise, then psychologically.

The rising curve of education is a fact. The "job appeal" curve is hypothetical, but it certainly exists in real life. The next chapter, "Why Jobs Die", states the case. Jobs must not be permitted to run down if American society is to meet the expectations of its young people. The very opposite must be true; jobs should challenge the more highly educated youngster of the future.

Why do youths expect to get good jobs if they stay in school? Because we tell them that's what will happen. I recall two public service advertising campaigns in New York City subway trains urging youths to stay in school. One was a simple table showing how much more one could expect to earn, on the average, for every additional year of education. The other was a placard saying in bold type:

> **Boy !** **THEY'LL ALWAYS CALL YOU "BOY"**
> **IF YOU DON'T STAY IN SCHOOL**
> **AND GET A GOOD EDUCATION.**

Expectations are transmitted by society. More money promised in the first placard, higher status in the second. These are associated by the young with the quality of the task they will be given if they stay in school. Society made the claim; now it's up to society to produce. If we are making millions of dull jobs, and if other jobs are eroding, we have a first-rate, long-range problem on our hands. For young people, especially members of minority groups, it is most important, first of all, that they get jobs. But for obvious reasons those jobs dare not be dull in the long run; they dare not be the kind of jobs that lead people to say, "I'd rather be on the street than doing this lousy job."

In the area of job quality as in so many areas of life, we have to run to stand still. Jobs will naturally deteriorate (see Chapter 2), or the introduction of changes will erode them. We must understand these processes and figure out how to offset them or be constantly unable to keep pace with employees' needs.

A Medical Slant on Task Satisfaction

No one would challenge the general idea that happy people live longer than unhappy people. There is now a striking bit of evidence that work satisfaction may have dramatic consequences for how long a person will live. Erdman Palmore of Duke University has been conducting a well-controlled study of life expectancy predictors and reports on the outcomes for 268 male and female, black and white volunteers, ages 60 to 94 at the start of the study in 1955.*

Thirty-nine items were studied for each person, many of which are thought to be tied to length of life. They include race, sex, various measures of health (blood pressure, use of tobacco), and how long one's ancestors lived. The study is still going on, but 233 records were complete at the time of Palmore's report in 1971. Discussion of the four items that best predicted life expectancy follows.

1. *Work satisfaction.* This was most important for the sample studied. "For the men in their 60's, work satisfaction could theoretically make a difference of up to nine years in longevity. . . . This work satisfaction score represents a person's reaction to his general usefulness and ability to perform a meaningful social role," writes Palmore. Subjects answered a series of printed questions in

*E. Palmore and F.C. Jeffers (eds.), *Prediction of Life Span,* Lexington, Mass.: D. C. Heath, 1971; see especially pp. 237–247.

order to allow the study team to score them as objectively as possible. If a person asked what was meant by "work," it was defined to include any useful activity such as housework, gardening, etc.

2. *Happiness.* Trained interviewers used a guided interview in arriving at a happiness rating. They worked without knowledge of the questionnaire results mentioned above. This was the second-best predictor of life expectancy among the study group.

3. *Physical functioning.* A physician rated all the subjects, using standard medical tests (blood, urine, electrocardiograms, and so on). Each subject's ratings were combined into a single score, which proved third best in predicting length of life.

4. *Use of tobacco.* As would be expected nowadays, the use of tobacco predicts a shorter life, a fact not too well known when this study was undertaken in 1955.

Dr. Palmore concludes his report with, "These findings suggest that, in general, the most important ways to increase longevity are: (1) to maintain a useful and satisfying role in society, (2) to maintain a positive view of life, (3) to maintain good physical functioning, and (4) to avoid smoking." Clearly, the two leading factors were social. I was surprised to find that the length of life of the subjects' parents had almost no relation to how long these people lived. I was not surprised to learn that length of life might be tied directly to job satisfaction. However, Dr. Palmore cautions that the case is far from proved.

The Exempt Organization

With the exception of the one-person company, where the individual does everything from meeting the customer/client to finishing the agreed-upon job, no organization is exempt from worry about job design. As soon as there is specialization of function among the members of the work group, the job design problem is also visible. Who will do what? How can we keep all of our group members, with their varying skills and abilities, functioning at an optimum level, one where they will be giving all they can give, not merely part of it?

The problem of employee motivation "bugs" managers of departments, especially large ones, to a greater extent than is generally recognized. It may not be the No. 1 problem of corporations, but it is certainly a persistent, attention-demanding problem. The sales records for reprints of the *Harvard Business Review* are evidence of this. This journal is read not only by managers of businesses but by government officials, educators, by almost anyone who runs a piece of an organization. The articles in any one issue may cover financing problems, accounting-auditing matters, sales and marketing, public relations, organizational strategies, and administrative skills, such as handling personnel problems. Readers may and do buy reprints of any articles that they wish to disseminate further, and their choices give us an interesting insight into what kind of article is most in demand.

Of the twelve most sought-after articles, ten deal with employee motivation or the leadership of employees (see the November–December 1977 issue). At the top, with sales of 735,000 reprints, is Frederick Herzberg's famous, "One More Time: How Do You Motivate Employees?" In it he presents his theory and reports on our first successful Bell System experiment, with a large group of well-educated but underutilized clerical workers, where he was the outside consultant. Scott Myers' article, "Who Are Your Motivated Workers?" stands third in reprint sales. Articles on how to lead and develop people are second and eleventh; both present motivational strategies. Performance appraisal is the subject of the ninth, tenth, and twelfth reprint leaders; clearly this is an employee motivational device as well as a salary administration item. Three others in the top twelve bear either upon administering or upon communicating within an organization. That leaves only two in the top twelve that do not deal directly with motivational matters. One deals with marketing and the other with salesmanship.

Managers have recognized the problem of motivation for a long time. They seek answers persistently. The articles and books keep coming, including mine. There is no final answer, of course, and few people expect one. But we must keep searching for better and better answers.

Certainly no organization should think itself exempt from concern over the problem of motivation. When employees go on strike, the issues are frequently economic, *but not always*. Furthermore, even an attempt to get more money, shorter hours, longer vacations, and so forth, can be a way of saying, "We hate being here." And strikes occur in all voluntary associations that I know of—corporations, universities, hospitals, government organizations, religious organizations.

I was reminded forcefully of the "no one is exempt" generalization when I was invited to the headquarters of a major American electrical workers' union in Washington, D.C., to talk about problems of job design and employee motivation. As we approached the building, my host said, "Oh, oh, we're being picketed today. Let's slip around to the side entrance."

"Who would dare picket a union?" I asked, as we avoided crossing the picket line.

"Our clerical people. We have trouble keeping them in this tight labor market. We often wish we didn't have to be located here. Maybe you'll have some ideas for us about these clerical jobs."

No doubt the clerical workers' union has its employee motivation problems too. Moving the headquarters out of town, to a place where there exists a grateful population, is probably only a stopgap solution. If job quality and the difficulty of retaining employees is a main problem, rather than the need for more space, lower taxes, access to a larger market or similar issues, then facing up to the task of *redesigning* jobs is likely to be the key to the solution. The "grateful" population out in "Wonderfultown" won't stay that way very long if they feel exploited. Even when people are paid reasonably well, if their abilities are underutilized, they will eventually feel that they are working only for money. And that's alienation from work.

No organization is exempt from the need for continuing surveillance of this problem, and no level in the organization is exempt. While lower-level supervisory jobs and staff assignments are especially prone to get into trouble, higher-level management jobs are far from being immune to the problem. So we must always ask: How good are our jobs? Are we keeping them good? What new equipment or procedure is coming along? What will it do to existing jobs? Can we seize upon the new situation as an opportunity to make jobs better while still reaping the other new advantages we expect? Soft music, a good cafeteria, a Christmas card personally signed by the boss, your birthday off as a personal holiday, all these are lovely. But they have nothing to do with the problem. And it is the problem that must be dealt with—directly.

No Time to Waste

In one sense there is no rush to get started. Like having a baby, it's going to take nine months anyhow—but a lot has to happen in those nine months. Likewise, it takes time to put a job design program into effect. So if you don't get started, the solution to the problem will be that much later in arriving. If you start now, you can expect to see results in six months to a year. This is not an unreasonable estimate of the time required to get results. Time flies while someone: finds the way to top management's ear; decides where and how to start; conducts seminars with managers so that they see the difference between this approach to motivation and traditional approaches; deals with and involves the unions, if they exist; initiates some field trials; gives the trials four to six months to take off.

Experience shows that this approach to motivation should be a way of life, not a one-shot program. Temporary programs can be mounted and dispatched, but not this effort. It is a philosophy of work, part of a philosophy of life.

Jobs Tend to Die

Any organization, especially an older one, may unknowingly have sick jobs, for the natural course of a job is for it to die at some time—unless steps are taken to prevent this from happening.

Jobs tend to die especially as a company or an organization grows in size, be it a government organization, a church, or a hospital. These are all meaningful, useful organizations, filled with high purpose at the start. Yet all of them carry within them the seeds of the destruction of their jobs.

I became acutely aware of this during one of the first Bell System experiments, wherein we enriched the job of the telephone service representative—the person who takes the customer's request to have a telephone installed, moved, or removed, and who gets after customers if they don't pay their bill. In the sessions where this job was reshaped in order to stop the loss of employees, the family of supervisors suggested ideas for improving the job. Some suggestions were to let the representative: (1) decide what a new customer's credit rating is, based on the evidence; (2) tell the customer whether a cash deposit is or is not necessary, and if it is necessary, how much it should be; (3) decide when to remind a customer about paying an overdue bill; (4) cut off the customer's service if the customer does not meet a deadline—no supervisory approval necessary; (5) decide whether an item on the customer's bill to which the customer objects is valid or not. These and other responsibilities were given to the employees. Such changes brought about declines in turnover of as much as 50 percent. Enormous savings in training costs and in the quality of service resulted.

When this success story was presented to the officers of the company, one said incredulously, "Why, I held that job myself back in the late 1930s and we had *all* those responsibilities. It was a great job! Whatever happened to it?"

In the next chapter, we'll look at what happens to jobs. Not all of today's poor jobs were good jobs to begin with, but jobs that were good at the outset can get sick and die if we don't discover the causes of the illness and figure out how to counteract them first.

2

---

why jobs die

WHEN ONE TRIES over a period of years to make dying jobs come back to life, one finally draws some conclusions as to what causes jobs to die. For about nine years I had no other corporate responsibility except to concentrate on and examine the quality of the work that people were asked to perform. Usually I and my staff were asked to look at a certain job for any of these reasons, or a combination of them:

1. Productivity was not what it could be.
2. Quality was down; too many errors.
3. Customers were complaining too much.
4. Departments were blaming each other.
5. Union relations were too tense, going far beyond the "adversary relation" level that is acceptable.
6. Employee quit rates rose as soon as job markets improved.
7. Training and inexperience were costly.
8. The bosses themselves felt there must be an easier way to run an organization.

This chapter tells why jobs get into trouble. There are 11 reasons, not necessarily clearly separate from each other. The illustrations of these reasons are taken from observations made while consulting on or observing a job situation, sometimes in corporations, sometimes in government or educational organizations. Where possible, I have chosen examples from outside the corporation where I worked.

Reason 1: Fragmentation

This is easily the main reason that jobs get worse. When a business is small, the owner has to do everything. The very success of businesses can lead to their undoing, as far as their jobs are concerned, for the owners start hiring other people to do parts of the job they once did all alone.

EXAMPLE 1—THE FRAMEROOM

In an attempt to improve the jobs of people who work in the telephone central office, we learned that a certain job, the frameman's job, was broken down as follows:

Person 1 takes the order for a private line or circuit from a customer, and when the private circuit is ready, contacts the customer again.
Person 2 figures out from engineering drawings how the loop should be laid out to meet the customer's need.
Person 3 writes a work order specifying the lugs and terminals to be connected.
Person 4 wires the circuit as directed.
Person 5 tests the circuit and tells Person 1 whether the circuit is okay.

These people are located in various parts of a 30-story building. Only rarely is all this work accomplished in a single eight-hour shift, for the work moves from person to person and place to place in stages.

All the people on this job were unionized and could eventually earn the same top-of-the-craft wages. There were no piece rates. Yet there were many problems in getting the circuit up correctly and on time. Productivity was low and grievances were many. Life was terrible for these craftspeople. For the bosses too.

The solution was: (1) Set up three-person teams and (2) give an order to a team, so that they could (3) talk to the customer, (4) lay out the loop, (5) write the work order, (6) perform the work, (7) test the circuit, and (8) call the customer back themselves, saying that the circuit was ready.

One of the older workers remarked, "We used to work this way; do it all. Then the war came along and we couldn't give customers the facilities they wanted. A backlog developed. We also lost a lot of our skilled people to the military service. When the war ended, someone figured we should break the job into five pieces. But no one is really responsible for putting up that circuit. Why, I've seen circuits fail to test out, and the night crew would straighten it out because the day people had gone home. The team that put the circuit up might never know that the circuit failed when it was tested. Now, we always know if the circuit's okay, and it's fun to tell the customer the circuit is ready."

Productivity and quality improved dramatically (for details, see *Motivation Through the Work Itself*). Equally important, so did the relations between employees and bosses. This whole job actually calls for the collaboration of about three people, because terminals can be on different floors and the craftspeople need to work simultaneously. To enrich this job, groups had to be formed that included workers with all the skills that were needed, and then they were given all the responsibility for completing an order. We often spoke of these as mini-groups. The fragments of work were returned to a group, in this case.

EXAMPLE 2—TYPEWRITER ASSEMBLY

In Amsterdam, Holland, IBM had a new typewriter assembly plant with two long, continuously moving assembly lines. No task took more than three minutes, a deliberate plan to reduce training time and, allegedly, to permit employees to develop skill and speed. More than a hundred people were on each continuous line. If trouble occurred, an accordion effect could be observed as the entire line shut down or speeded up. Productivity was considerably below the expectations of the industrial engineers, quality problems arose constantly, costs were too high, and there was talk of moving this new plant elsewhere to meet the rising demand for the product.

The managers broke up the long lines into shorter, M-shaped lines, which enabled people in the middle legs of the M to turn and tell people at other stages what, if anything, was going wrong. Every person had to learn and perform two, three, or four stages in typewriter assembly, increasing the cycle time to ten minutes.

Some human consequences emerged. The mini-lines, as they were called, were so short—about 20 people—that the many different language groups in that particular plant could be accommodated. New employees and trainees could work on a slower line, as could handicapped people, which all employers are required by law to hire. Different products could be assigned to mini-lines more easily, as could typewriters destined for a particular foreign country with its particular language. Lines could shut themselves to meet their own preferences for the regular coffee breaks. Cafeterias were utilized better. Lines could decide to start earlier and leave earlier, or to start later and leave later. There was less crowding in parking lots and on buses.

All of this occurred, plus improvements in productivity and quality. Labor turnover, which had been 30 percent annually, dropped dramatically. Unnecessary fragmentation had had many negative consequences. When I observed the lines in 1973, three years after the first redesign,* they were still undergoing change in the new

*Note that I am referring to the concepts in this book as "job design and work organization." Specifically, however, job design refers to the development of new jobs and job redesign refers to the reshaping of existing jobs.

direction, toward more wholeness of work. They were even setting up micro-lines within the mini-lines, where individuals could make whole subassemblies if they wished and test them out themselves, thus eliminating the need for a separate test station. Many of the work groups were beginning to handle their own administration, as well as formerly centralized tasks such as parts ordering.

To be sure, the increase in productivity resulting from this job redesign effort was partly due to the fact that the typewriters simply didn't have to move around as much during assembly as before. But the psychological effects of "de-fragmentation" were at least as important. Instead of forcing workers to adapt themselves to a set task, the new system adapts the work to the needs of the employees. As a result, the reason cited for leaving the company now tends to be the need for better housing, for example, rather than, "I don't want to be a robot for the rest of my life."[†]

EXAMPLE 3—DIRECTORY COMPILATION

Here is the most spectacular case of unnecessary fragmentation of work. In the Indiana Bell Telephone Company, about 35 clerks were assigned to 21 different jobs for getting new names into the new telephone directories that come out once a year for each city in the state. There are about 58 directories. When the last one emerges, the whole cycle begins again. Customers' names and yellow-pages advertisers are continually being added or dropped. The problem: too many errors, too many employees quitting, too much training, too many complaints from customers, especially advertisers, about receiving their directories late. Management was unhappy, and an attitude survey revealed that the employees were unhappy too. And if you were a customer whose name was

[†]For more detailed accounts of this job redesign effort, see Nancy Foy, "A Blow at the Factory Automaton," *The Times* (London), March 5, 1973, and Tom Wicker, "The Work and the Worker," *The New York Times*, June 18, 1974.

misspelled, you were probably none too happy yourself.

A glance at the "Before Work Itself" column in Figure 2 reveals one problem: almost every other station or step involved a "checker." On the basis of observations in other studies of jobs in trouble, a decision was made to eliminate checking for any employees who had enough training to check their own work. The middle column in the figure shows the first change—dropping from 21 stations to 14. This difference alone brought good results and much greater employee cooperation.

The truly dramatic column is the third one, which shows all 21 stations reduced to one. A single clerk became responsible for getting out three directories; another had four directories—whole pieces of work. "A book of my own," these clerks would say.

Figure 2. Work itself as a motivator.

Indiana Bell Telephone Company
Directory Compilation Project

Job Titles and Work Assignments Before and After

Before Work Itself	Phase I — Work Itself	Phase II — Work Itself
White Pages:	White Pages:	Clerk 1 TOTAL DIRECTORY
Clerk 1 1103 Clerk	Clerk 1 1103 Clerk	One Book-One Clerk
" 2 Manuscript Clerk	" 2 Manuscript Clerk	Performs all functions except Keytape.
" 3 Manuscript Checker		
Yellow Pages:	Yellow Pages:	
Clerk 4 Mail Desk	Clerk 3 Mail Desk	
" 5 Quality Control		
" 6 Analyst	" 4 Analyst	
" 7 Checker		
" 8 Keypunch	" 5 Keytape	
" 9 Keypunch Verifier		
" 10 Manuscript Clerk	" 6 Manuscript Clerk	
" 11 Manuscript Checker		
" 12 Ad Copy Clerk	" 7 Ad Copy Clerk	
" 13 Ad Copy Checker		
" 14 Customer Proof Clerk	" 8 Customer Proof Clerk	
" 15 Manila Control Clerk	" 9 Manila Control Clerk	
" 16 Look-Up Clerk	" 10 Look-Up Clerk	
" 17 NYPS Clerk	" 11 NYPS Clerk	
" 18 NYPS Checker		
" 19 Biller	" 12 Biller	
" 20 Error Control Clerk	" 13 Error Control Desk	
" 21 Transfer Desk	" 14 Transfer Desk	

For a large directory, such as the one for Indianapolis, the supervisors could assign portions of the alphabet to individuals, who could aspire to handle whole books in time, if they wished. Planning and talking with clerks and training them to perform all the steps in producing a whole directory took about a year. New pay grades were established for employees who accepted the new responsibilities and who performed well. The unions cooperated. Quitting to go elsewhere almost disappeared. Movement up the ladder became common, as the clerks displayed competence and responsibility, qualities that had not been readily discernible when they worked in a 21-step production line. Clerks in some locations were permitted to come to work early, leave early, and go on breaks when they elected, because their work did not affect the work of other clerks.

The "one person–one book" example is a classic illustration of how to eliminate the negative consequences of fragmentation of work. The 21 steps were indeed the steps needed to produce a telephone directory with its white and yellow pages, but 21 different people did not have to do them. It is a matter of record that some error-free directories have been produced under the new approach, as the idea spread to other companies of the Bell System. A manager in Birmingham said, "I have eight directories here about which no one has reported an error, not one customer complaint, not one dollar refunded for a mistake in an advertisement. This is a directory manager's dream." It is a lesson about job fragmentation too. (For more details about this project, see the Appendix.)

EXAMPLE 4—FANCY DINING ROOM

Recently we attended a conference at a hotel in San Juan, Puerto Rico—which was on the beach and bankrupt too, I was told. But elegant. The employees wore many kinds of uniforms of different colors, with and without stripes and braid. At lunch time one day we wanted only a quick, light meal. We went to the main dining room, where we were attended by the following people:

1. The receptionist/reservation person. "Do you have a reservation (for a seat in our nearly empty dining room)?" "No." After much scanning of a book, "Okay, follow me please," and she raised her hand.
2. The headwaiter, who took us 15 feet into the dining room where he raised a hand.
3. The captain of an area in the dining room, who seated the three of us and gave us menus.
4. The set-up person, who removed the extra setting from the table and poured water for us.
5. The bar waiter, who appeared from his corner of the room to ask if we wished something to drink. "No, not now."
6. The waiter, who asked, "Oh, are you having nothing to drink?" and then took our orders.
7. The bus boy, who removed any plate or dish we had finished with, once the waiter called it to his attention.
8. An unknown boy in a black coat, very short in the back, and black pants with black stripes down the outseams, who did not provide any service but stood nearby. He was probably an apprentice—at what I don't know.

No doubt, there were half a dozen different employees in the kitchen, such as salad chef, sandwich chef, meat chef, vegetable chef, chef chef, but they are not counted here due to lack of verification, nor are the dishwashers, pot washer, silverware washer, etc., counted.

One of the conferees, a Puerto Rican accountant, informed us that the hotel literally had more employees than guests at any one time. The reason we chatted about such things is that we had an unbelievable amount of time between meeting the receptionist and receiving our coffee. So much for the quick, light meal we'd wanted. Perhaps this is elegant living; it certainly is a slow-motion example of work fragmentation. I would speculate that these workers do not like their jobs, despite their various uniforms and symbols of status, that there are many quarrels about who is supposed to do what, especially when an irate customer finally snaps at someone: "Say, where is my sandwich?" Who is responsible in a chain like that?

The waiter's job can be a satisfying one, no doubt about it. The answer is not having one person who does everything from opening the restaurant to washing the dishes. Some fragmentation is desirable, but it can go berserk.

EXAMPLE 5—TEACHING

Older people, whose educational experience is ancient history, may not realize the extent to which the job of educating children can be fragmented. In a consolidated school district just north of New York City, I was informed during a seminar on how to motivate teachers to do a good job, "like they did in the old days," that many responsibilities have been shorn from the classroom teacher. Here are some examples:

Testing—standard tests used by all teachers, drawn up outside the consolidated school district.
Curriculum—in detail, determined outside the district.
Visual aids—many from outside, with separate specialists within the district to fetch materials.
Textbook selection—outside the district.
Counseling—a specialized service within the district.
Paper grading—automatic, or performed by assistants.
Difficult disciplinary cases—a specialized service run by trained persons within the district.
Students' after-school activities—all conducted by specialists, coaches; no teacher participation.
Continuing teacher education—a mandatory program from outside the district, with certification as to courses completed and degrees attained as the key to salary progress rather than performance in educating children.

This model for educating is a far cry from the ideas of the American philosopher and educator Mark Hopkins, who stated that the best education in the world is between a person and a child on opposite ends of a log. Who *is* responsible in a complex, fragmented system when a child fails to learn? The school psychologist? Perhaps there aren't enough teachers and logs to go around, but the opposite approach—minute division of labor—is not the answer either.

Reason 2: Job Specifications

Job fragmentation is the leading culprit. It leads to written specifications, "jobs specs," as trouble breaks out, and trouble will break out, thanks to the fragmentation. In trying to improve jobs, workers repeatedly run into "job specs" as the reason that job changes cannot be made. The "specs" forbid the contemplated move. Fortunately, in the frameman and directory clerk examples, the jobs were not defined by *written* specs, which helped a lot when we redesigned them.

If the jobs have written specifications, and employees really get mad at the boss, the company, or the government, the easiest way for them to shut down operations—as they did with the British railroads and the New York City subways—is to "go by the book." Or in the trucking industry, if there is a rule that says, "Obey speed limits," the easiest way for the trucker to strike back at the boss who wants the furniture delivered in Florida when he promised the family it would be there is to obey that 55 mile limit. Or if the trucker has worked his eight- or ten-hour shift and he's on the edge of that Florida town, forget it! Pull into a motel for the night.

The easiest way for air controllers to make known their grievances is to go by the book. Perhaps the controllers could let planes land every $1\frac{1}{2}$ minutes if they tend to their business carefully. But the book says that they are to keep airplane safety in the forefront of their consciousness at all times. Therefore let them land 4 or 5 minutes apart. Those of us who have circled an airport while air controllers made their point know firsthand what job specifications can do to the customer's insides.

At the time he was president of the Carnegie Foundation, John W. Gardner, psychologist, philosopher, and all-around sage, remarked, "The final act of a dying organization is to rewrite and enlarge the rule book." Obviously, imposing rigid rules and job specifications is the wrong way to approach job performance problems. Rather, we should ask ourselves, How can we design jobs and rule books that are compatible? How can we formulate rules with which we can live, which are as changeable and flexible as the situations in which work must be done?

Reason 3: Perfect Practices

The "perfect practice" is unlike the written job specification in that it is unwritten and carries with it the expectation that it will die with the end of the particular service campaign or sales drive. For example, customer representatives of a certain airline were trained to smile as customers stepped up to the representative's position. And a smile was not accepted as a smile unless the company's service observer could see the flash of an employee's teeth. This was considered a fair and objective test of an appropriate smile—whether or not the bicuspids had been displayed.

It's hard to find fault with the motivation behind this practice; the company wanted to be known as a friendly company. But how did it work out? One employee was challenged by the service observer. He had noted on his clipboard that the employee had not smiled; in fact, she had looked displeased with the customer. The employee said that that was right indeed! That was the third time the drunken bum had annoyed her about his tickets, and not only did she not smile then, but she would never smile unless she felt like it. And if the company didn't like it, they could take their job and . . . . .

Interviews with employees reveal consistently that

they hate speeches that are "pasted on the end of my tongue." Customer service representatives in a small town claimed that they were asked to try to sell an extension telephone in addition to the main station to every customer calling to obtain new service. The extra revenue to the company would be welcome indeed, and there would be prizes for those who sold the most extensions. As part of the training, they were instructed to raise the question *at least twice* in every contact. And management felt that a third attempt would demonstrate real employee hustle.

Here is one representative's experience with this practice. She received a call for new service. The customer agreed to install a green telephone at the end of the sofa in his living room. Then she asked, in line with the new practice, "How about a nice green extension in the kitchen?" The customer said he did not have a kitchen; it was a one-room efficiency apartment. As her second attempt, she countered, "Why not install an extension in the bathroom?" The customer said, "No, indeed." As her third and final attempt, the representative claims she asked, "How about an extension for the other end of the sofa!" Although they both laughed, she offered this practice as a job liability.

Perfect practices are not always designed merely to make money for the company. Sometimes they are conceived as the way to give good service. A man claimed that his bill arrived from a department store just as he was rushing out of his house for Kennedy Airport in New York on his way to Paris. He noticed that he had been overcharged precisely $100 for a piece of luggage he had bought, probably a mere slip-up—a nervous finger had accidentally touched a wrong button. But in view of his six-week trip, he did not want to get tarred with a "bad credit" brush. He called the store from an airport phone booth, having waited in line to use the phone. The dimes disappeared as he reached "Luggage," and was passed to "Customer Relations," and finally to "Bookkeeping."

The clerk in bookkeeping got the point and said that she would get the records and call right back. What is the telephone number there? The customer said that he did not dare hang up because there was a line of people outside the booth waiting impatiently to use the phone.

Again the clerk insisted on calling back, because she knew it would take five minutes to get the record, and she was required to call him back rather than keep him on the line that long. Again the man insisted that he had enough dimes to feed the coinbox, and begged her to get the records while he waited. Again she said she couldn't.

Finally he exploded, shouting that he was the customer and he wanted her to get the records. To which she replied, "I don't work for you, I work for the comapny."

The customer gave her the telephone number and angrily stood his ground against the line outside the booth.

The company intent was excellent: Don't keep customers hanging on the line if you have reason to think you will be away for more than $1\frac{1}{2}$ minutes. That was the rule, and the clerk was obeying it to the letter. No doubt both sides hated that perfect practice, but let's concern ourselves for a moment with this seemingly obstinate employee—who is trying to do a good job. Her service was being monitored and she knew it, so she had no choice but to follow the rule and watch the quality of her job die in the process. Her angry response to the customer says in effect, "This situation is ridiculous, but my hands are tied."

Reason 4: Perfect Training

In my earliest studies of force loss or quitting I learned that training itself can cause people to quit their jobs. Too often, training can be overtraining.

"Oh, another of those damn training courses! Here we go again. It will be 'How to Prevent Errors' or 'The Importance of Preventing Errors.' Something like that, you'll see," is the frequent reaction.

As was revealed in the directory compilation example, where almost every other task was a check on the previous task, the solution was not further training in error prevention but thorough training of employees just once on how to check the accuracy of their work. Next, the stage was set so that they *wanted* to prevent errors. How? Through the expedient of assigning whole books to individuals, so they could take pride in doing a complete job and doing it very well.

In our first successful trial at redesign work in the Bell System, we learned that there was a three-week training period before fledgling correspondents were allowed to write a letter—and then the boss got to sign it. Over the first year, this training was not cut out, but it was changed so that correspondents could write a single letter about a single problem the first day on the job—and sign their name to it.

Yes, it was hard on the boss, who had to answer the question, "Just what is my job, my *distinct* job, as opposed to that of my correspondents?" Surely it is not that of reading and signing all their outgoing mail. "I guess I should be counseling them on tough problems and training them on problems they're ready to learn to solve." The bosses were quite willing to do this on-the-job training.

But at first they had no time for such training, as they were trying to do too much of the employees' job. Add to this the fact that they were usually short-staffed, because the job of correspondent had a high turnover rate.

The training school for correspondents had indeed been a busy place because of this loss of employees. Material was frequently added to the curriculum as new problems arose, so that the correspondents would be perfectly trained when they arrived on the job. I recall two despairing comments made by supervisors in a discussion of that training situation: "Have you ever noticed that training courses get longer, never shorter?" and "The problem is becoming: how to get prospective correspondents to survive this training school. A lot of fine young people drop out before they really start on the job. Isn't there some way we could get them on to the job faster?"

Perhaps an army must train perfectly for meeting every eventuality before going into battle, because lives are at stake. This seldom applies to a business, where the new employee can say to the boss or to another person in the mini-group, "What do I do now?" I have been amazed to see, when a strike occurred and management people were thrust into unfamiliar jobs everywhere, that everything is immediately shorn from the training but the bare essentials. In a strike situation, a *day* of training might be long for some jobs. In many cases the key training procedure would simply be placing beginners alongside experienced people. All kinds of cross-talk are permitted then, in violation of the former perfect practice, which prohibited talking between positions, even about job problems.

A recent private study of requests from line organizations for help in training in a large corporation revealed that 80 percent of the requests could not be substantiated on grounds that knowledge or skill was actually lacking. Instead, the training request resulted from other defects in the flow of work and how the job slices were arranged. Enough knowledge and skill were found to be present if work flows were changed appropriately. Training is usually expensive, and overtraining or the training of too many people is inexcusable.

Reason 5: Departmentalization

Departmentalization of work may be a necessary evil, but employees often don't like it, and it can kill good performance. In the hotel example cited earlier, I found the first morning that I could not shave properly because a fluorescent tube had burned out in the bathroom. Since I had four more days to go, I left a note on the mirror requesting a new bulb.

Day 2 was as bad as Day 1—still no bulb.

No bulb on Day 3. I stopped the maid in the hall, took

her to the room, and pointed to the burned-out bulb. Although there was a language problem, her "Si, si" indicated that she understood the problem.

On Day 4, after I had shaved in semidarkness, a man entered and most graciously changed the bulb. As I was preparing to check out, I discovered his multicopy work order lying on the floor. It contained white, green, and orange sheets, each to go to different places. That was the culprit; someone had sold the hotel on departmentalization of work. The Job Request for the Engineering Department, # 1441 (I still have it, probably fouling up their accounting system too) stated that Room 424 wanted a light bulb. The order read, "□ phoned by J.D."—I presume the maid.

The next signature is under "Housekeeping," with more initials, to be sure. Then the order was logged in by "Engineering at 11:45 A.M." Next, this work was "Assigned to LaCosta." Finally, the order read, "Work checked by _____," but this had no initials on it, for, I'm afraid, LaCosta had lost the work order.

One light bulb!

There is no apparent reason why the maid could not have a collection of light bulbs so that she could replace burned-out bulbs herself. Then she could replenish her stock by trading in the burned-out bulbs. Replacing an open, exposed fluorescent tube is not really difficult.

Interviews show that employees do not like to hand over a customer to someone else if they can handle the problem themselves. They learn to say with asperity, "Don't call me, call repair service," only because they know they have to handle the problem that way. Most employees in our studies tended to want to help customers. Departmentalization was frequently the cause of bad customer contacts, not bad employees. Human beings are always learning what they are supposed to do, and if they don't like it, they may become defensive and obnoxious. The system sets it off, not the employee.

Reason 6: The Instant Rule

The flash reaction to a bad situation, the "instant rule," can easily erode employees' jobs and their feeling of being responsible people. This was clearly demonstrated in one of our attempts to improve the quality of jobs. The effort was moving slowly, poorly. The time had come to call the supervisors together in an effort to stimulate their interest.

I was informed that our Monday morning meeting would be delayed for half an hour because the supervisors were conducting a safety hearing. One of their small trucks had been hit by a motorist in front of the company's garage on the previous Friday night at quitting time, and the driver of their truck had been ordered to appear for a hearing at the garage. He appeared in sports clothing, eager to take off on his vacation, which was being delayed by this hearing. I was invited to sit in on the inquiry, after which the regular meeting would start. Forty minutes of hearing, with the big boss from downtown serving as chairman, boiled down to this:

"So, we've lost the Division Safety Trophy for August. What happened? What's your version?"

"Sir, I was turning left in front of the garage last Friday night, to turn in my truck, when this guy ran through a red light at the corner and plowed into my right door."

"Were you arrested?"

"No, he was, not I. I think he was drunk. He had to take a drunkometer test, they said. I only had to make out an accident report at the police station, but they put him in a cell for a while."

"You know there goes the Division Safety Trophy, don't you?"

"Yes, sir. I'm sorry."

"Well, accidents don't happen; they're caused. Tell me now, what time did you say this happened, exactly?"

"About ten minutes before five, quitting time, sir."

"Do you mean to tell me you were making a left turn off

DeSoto Street at five o'clock? Where are your brains? That's a busy street. From now on, you supervisors, I don't want any left turns made off DeSoto Street between four-fifteen and six-thirty in the evening. No turns at all. And while we're at it, I don't want any left turns between those hours off the other two streets leading to this garage, Howard and Dupont Streets. Is that clear?"

One of the other drivers called this the "instant rule book." He said, "I've driven a truck for 17 years and I've never had even one accident. And now I can't turn left off DeSoto Street. Just like I was a kid."

The tale did not end there. With cynical glee, a driver told me three months later, "Now do you know what happened? We had *another* accident in front of the garage." The driver looked at his watch and said, "Thank God, it's seven o'clock! Honest to God, he did!"

The instant rule can damage not only the employee but the employee–boss relationship. One public utility had evening and night trouble-shooter repairmen. This was a specially skilled and somewhat more dangerous assignment than the corresponding daylight hours job. It paid better and was available to senior employees especially, if they wished.

Unfortunately, one night a repairman was caught peeping through a bedroom window, and the police arrested him. His trial was scheduled for a few weeks later, and an immediate order went out, "Every supervisor will routinely visit every night crewman once a week. But don't do it on a regular schedule so that they won't know when to expect you."

I can just hear the following dialog taking place:

"Hi, boss, what the hell brings you out on a night like this? I haven't seen you out here in my area in ten months, I'll bet. What's up?"

"Well, Sam, you may be an incipient Peeping Tom, so I thought..."

No, the foreman was too smart to say that, but the fact is that almost anything the boss says will cause estrangement with these senior skilled craftspeople. The instant rule has caused this top-of-the-craft job to die a little. Autonomy is one facet of a job that employees like.

The concept of self-canceling rules has not caught on in most organizations—rules that automatically expire in 30 days unless the big boss acts again. By this time the boss might be feeling better about not getting the division trophy or about the undoubtedly adverse publicity surrounding the "Peeping Tom" incident, so the new rule might be quietly forgotten.

Reason 7: Authority Moves Up

When anything goes wrong in an organization, authority is likely to move up, leaving the job level below to die a little bit.

I first noticed this when, with obvious delight, a supervisor told this tale:

The boss played golf weekly with three business acquaintances, one of whom claimed his telephone bill had many overcharges each month. How did he know? Because he had hired a consulting service to check his monthly bill for a share of the savings, and the consultant had turned up 42 errors in the previous month's bill.

The telephone boss could hardly believe this, so he asked that the bill and the alleged errors be studied by his own supervisors. The supervisors agreed with the consulting firm on many, but not all, items, and even found 9 more errors themselves, all small, but they were there. The boss was incensed. He ordered, "From now on, pull the bill for my buddy before it goes out and send it to my desk. And while you're at it, send the bills for the other two guys I play golf with also, since they know this story now."

After a careful check on each of the three bills, they went to the boss. He reviewed them and then stuffed the three in the wrong envelopes and mailed them!

Authority had moved up, as it does every time the boss

takes over a responsibility that properly belongs with a subordinate. The boss now deserves the big briefcase that will need to be taken home each evening. It's too bad that someone made an error or overspent the budget, but the movement of authority upward is not the answer.

Employees will learn how to defeat the boss in order to keep the business running. If the formal limit for an equipment purchase is $500, don't buy a new desk and chair, for that would run $510. Buy a desk, and then buy a chair on a separate requisition—an old game in a bureaucracy, for that's what the boss is establishing. A bureau is a place run by a rule book. Money cutoff points tend to cause jobs to die because economic inflation cuts down the range of decision making all by itself. When all typewriters finally cost over $500, or whatever the limit might be, the boss has in effect decreed, "No one can buy typewriters anymore. I want this authority exclusively."

As the boss's briefcase finally bulges beyond belief, the boss can easily cement this unfortunate upward movement into place. How? By appointing a special assistant for budget items—reporting directly to the boss. Now there is a new "half-level" job, halfway between the supervisors and the boss. Try to get rid of that job after it's been there three or four years! The very purpose of a budget has been defeated: instead of minimizing costs, an unnecessary job, with its associated salary and overhead costs, has been created.

The outflow of money must be watched; that's not the issue. The issue is this: Who is to do it, without robbing job occupants who legitimately had this responsibility? When a new level is sandwiched in, all the jobs below it are reduced, psychologically if not economically. When errors occur, when expenses appear to be getting out of hand, whenever the boss makes any move to "tighten up the ship," the organization is beginning to make death rattles. A vibrant, healthy organization, one that is growing, is one where you might hear, "Look, Marion, from now on you handle all of these accounts. Everybody can't be in on this any longer. Just let me know when you see trouble brewing and let me know long enough in advance so that you and I can plan our way out of it. I'll hold you responsible for that. Okay?" The healthy organization is one where the boss gives away authority. Those who handle it best will be the boss's successors, well trained for the job through firsthand experience.

Reason 8: Fun and Excitement Removed

The only excitement in a firefighter's job, I imagine, comes when there is a fire. The rest of the time, the job is one of drilling, studying, cleaning the equipment, polishing the truck, and waiting. In a real sense every good job has some fun and excitement in it, something interesting occasionally, a problem to be solved, figuring out how to get something working again or what to do about a mass of unsold inventory.

The fun of a switchboard operator's job may well be calling an ambulance, putting a call through to the police, helping an elderly person or a young child reach someone by telephone. The surest way to kill that job is by saying to operators, "The moment there is an emergency call of any kind, hit this 'panic button' and a service assistant will cut in and take over while you return to your regular calls." On those unfortunate days when I, as a management person, was assigned to a switchboard because of a walkout, I was mighty glad that a service assistant was there, for I knew so little. But if that job were my full-time, lifetime work, and if I were never able to call the cops myself, I could rightly feel like an eternal beginner.

When people who maintain the telephone plant, central offices, outside cables, and other heavy equipment get together for a beer after a long absence from each other, what do they talk about? "Hey, do you remember that power blackout when one of our own electric generators failed to kick in! What a night, getting that thing running and keeping it running, or we would have had a telephone blackout as well." The high spots of their careers so often center on snowstorms, cable failures, events that were out of the ordinary.

A high point of my early career occurred the morning I was in a garage of the Bell System and the drivers were leaving in an unhappy mood about some new ruling that the boss had just passed along to the troops. When the last grumpy driver had left, the boss said almost to himself, "Lord, give us a snowstorm." "Why would you want a snowstorm?" I asked. His thoughtful reply ran along these lines: "Then, if ever, is when we work best, most willingly, and with good feeling. Would I give them hell if I caught them in a diner drinking coffee in the middle of the night during a snowstorm? No, sir, I'd join them and probably pay the bill. Can you believe this: Our records show that our safety performance is at its very best when the hazards are greatest. Everyone is paying attention to what they are doing."

Fun can't be manufactured, but if there is fun in a job—problems, puzzles, difficult things to handle—it must not be removed on the grounds that "This isn't your job. We need you over there. Let this go and I'll do it." Consider the fun as sacred to a job. The surest way to empty the nation's golf courses would be to insist that a club pro be stationed every hundred yards to shoot any difficult shots, so that golf balls wouldn't get into the town drinking water, so that passing autos wouldn't get clobbered, so that the turf wouldn't get dug up by duffers. The art of making a good golf course is just the opposite. Design some natural problems into it, and let the players solve them. Job designers can well take a lesson from this.

Reason 9: Measurement Plans

A repairman came to our home at the appointed time to fix the washing machine. As he was finishing, I said, "Would you also look at the dryer? It seems to take entirely too long to dry clothes, and then they aren't dry enough." He replied, "I can't touch it without a work order. Call our service desk and make an appointment. I'm always around here somewhere." As you might guess, a brief controversy ensued. I had already incurred the flat $16 fee for a house call, and I merely wanted to buy more time. He blamed the company. We both lost emotionally, I'm afraid.

Chances are that a "measurement plan" was taking over the company. Someone wanted to be sure that orders were written properly, timed properly, priced properly, billed properly, collected properly, properly, properly. But here were a fine craftsperson and a fairly reasonable customer—both somewhat upset, to be sure.

How to get out of this? Earlier studies of Bell Systems craftspeople had shown similar problems. We had learned that craftspeople can and should be supplied with their own order books, be told to write up the orders and get the customers to sign them, perform the work, and turn the completed work orders in at the end of the day. One can imagine, in fact, rewarding employees for turning up more work rather than ordering them to refuse it.

I can imagine objections, such as, "The craftspeople don't know all the symbols, all the shorthand used in writing up orders. After all, a computer is involved also. They'll have to be trained." The first craftsperson I asked about that drawback shot back, "I can *read* the symbols, why can't I *write* them too?"

Another objection could be, "We've given them a full day's work now. They can't add other jobs on their own." An amazing revelation, to the contrary, was that craftspeople could easily handle small additional requests if they wanted to. And if my repairman could not handle more work on that day, or if he ran into a real mess when he opened up the clothes dryer, he could at least have scheduled this work himself. As he said, "I'm always around here somewhere." Part of the fun of a job is scheduling the work yourself.

In one of our studies, before craftspeople had their own

"turf," their own area within a certain city, a complaint was made that one man was often seen in a diner right after he arrived on his turf. His rejoinder was, "You still route me, you don't let me route myself. And you route me into the X Apartments first thing, every time, because they're closest to the garage on my turf. But that superintendent is never there until 8:30 A.M., so what am I to do? Argue with the guy who does the routing. That's his job, I'm told. If you were smart, now that I have my own turf, you'd let me route myself."

This man was also one of the first to get his own order book. Under the "turf" arrangement, he built up enough friendships with apartment building superintendents that one day he proudly displayed a ring of keys enabling him to get into almost all apartment houses, office buildings, and equipment rooms on his turf. This was accomplished because work measurement plans were revised, redesigned. His work was still "measured," of course, but in such a way as to keep his job vital.

On production jobs, work measurement plans can easily be self-defeating: (1) If the number of parts made or assembled is the criterion, the worker ignores the quality. (2) If the number of calls handled is the criterion, the worker cuts off the customer who wants to say something pleasant, to chat. (3) If the rule is "publish or perish" for university faculty promotion, professors turn scholarly efforts into a production line. Get out the articles and books; don't fuss with quality.

Every job, from lowest to highest, can be spoiled by oppressive measurement plans. In redesigning jobs, we learned to teach employees to log their own productivity and also the quality. Quality cannot always be measured objectively; sometimes it is simply a matter of counting letters of praise or complaint from customers on one's turf. Measurement is important. The problem is to get it into the hands of the right person, the employee who is being measured.

Reason 10: De-skilling

When soldering guns were being phased out in a plant that was producing sound amplifiers, superiors noted that the new wire wrapping guns were resisted by many employees. They were losing a skill—"Any dummy can use that electric wire wrapper to make the connections," workers said. To offset the loss, the amount of work each person performed on the amplifier was increased. The objective was to let a person wire the entire "front end," or the entire "final stage." With this change in objective, one could hear an employee say, "I never have a bad connection now that we've gone from soldering to wire wrapping."

As part of this effort to block de-skilling, the employees were taught how to test their part of the amplifier. Even though this called for more equipment than was previously needed, the overall improvement in productivity and quality more than offset the cost of the wire wrapping guns, additional equipment, longer training time, and possibly lower speed on any given step in the cycle. The individual steps might indeed be more costly; however, the system was more productive as a whole.

An understanding that de-skilling tends to kill jobs is especially necessary at the critical moment when new equipment or tools are on the threshold and jobs are going to be changed. It is not sufficient for the experts to be steeped in the new technology (for example, the cathode ray tubes, the computer, the word processing center, the new electronic search apparatus for scanning a central office for defective circuits). They are not truly experts unless they also understand the needs of the people at work. Consider this illustration from the directory compilation discussed earlier in this chapter. Recall that this success story involved a reduction in the number of people working on a particular directory so that, ideally, one person–one directory resulted.

Everyone was happy until a new project came along, wherein customers' names, addresses, and telephone numbers were to be stored in a computer permanently, or at least until the customer made a change. Under this system, once a year, the button would be pressed and out would come a copy for all the white pages, if not the yellow pages, without anyone's laying a finger on paper records. This change brought with it a near tragedy so far as employees' jobs were concerned. No one in research and development knew about the one book–one person effort. Innocently enough, with computerization, the new job titles were to be (with only a bit of exaggeration): message receipt clerk, message opening clerk, coding scrubber clerk, directory input clerk, input verification clerk, etc., etc. Lots of verification clerks, of course. The information for all cities in a state would be stored in one computer, all clerks would be attached to it, and no directory would be produced by only one person.

In actual practice now, the old and the new are melded. The employees who had their own directories still have them. Instead of working with paper, they were trained to work with a computer input terminal. They now have a better tool to accomplish the old, desirable job of providing a whole directory for a city. On woman is quoted as saying, "When I produced my own directory, all by myself, I just floated." That is the "something" that must not get lost when new tools or equipment threaten to deskill.

After hearing this story during a seminar in northern France, the manager of a large, successful yarn factory invited us to see a living example of his own. In the packaging room the beautifully dyed yarn was spun into balls, about 20 spindles per machine, with its operator. When enough yarn was on the spindle, the operator would stop the machine, quickly place an attractive paper band around each ball, cut the yarn with a quick motion at a severing lever, yank each ball off the spindle, and pack them all neatly in boxes. While packing the box and opening a new one, the operator pushed another lever and the spindles ran again until full. That was the operator's job: Get a box ready, start the spindles, stop the spindles, band the yarn, cut the yarn, remove the yarn, pack the yarn, start the machine, get a box, and so on.

We had had this described to us prior to entering the noisy room. I was prepared to see sad-looking workers, crushed by their fate. When the door opened, operators glanced at us as their hands flew at the banding-packaging job. The young woman nearest the door, quite in contrast to my expectation, started a "dance" with her machine. Although many levers were obviously designed to be pushed by hand, she pushed as many of the low ones as possible with little kicks of her feet. This enabled her to work faster, for she reserved the use of her hands for removing and packing the balls of yarn. The boss laughed as she laughed. This was apparently an old joke, and he had deliberately elected to take us into the room through the door nearest her machine. This employee and her machine were on good terms with each other.

"Now," he said, "I want you to see my problem. It is not the machines you just saw, but the three new ones from Switzerland, top-of-the-art machines, latest and best in the world. Each of them does all of the things you saw that young woman do."

Sure enough, each machine took a reel of yarn, wound off just enough for a ball, automatically banded the ball of yarn, moved it toward a box, placed each ball where there was space in the box, closed and sealed the box when the last space was filled, moved it away, and placed an empty box on the loading tray. The production rate and costs were such that the machines operated by humans had to be phased out.

"What is the problem?" I asked innocently.

"We have trouble with the people who tend these three machines," said our host. "Their job is to see that the machines do not stop, that the yarn is quickly retied should it break. They are to place a stack of bands here, where the balls are automatically banded, and to be sure there are enough boxes for the balls of yarn to be packed in. They hate this job. Would you believe they actually fall asleep while standing there? We used to let them sit, but that's out. When they sit, they fail to see when the yarn breaks; they fail to keep the band tray full, and the balls go unbanded into the box; they forget to load empty boxes in the rack, and the balls fall on the floor. How can I enrich this job?"

I certainly had no quick answer. I asked lamely, "Have you talked to the three operators about the problem? Why do they neglect the machines?"

"They say that they want to go back to the other spindle room, where they can kick the levers and dance around! But we want to phase out the rest of the old spindles for economic reasons. What do I do about this job?"

The spindle operator's job was dying. The new one required no skill. There is no easy answer. Perhaps the machine designers should go still further in automation, virtually eliminating human operators. One tender could then tend a group of machines.

Enriching the final fragment of a job is not easy. The computer, especially, is prone to leaving only a fragment of a once tough job. In one instance, clerks in the Bell System had to be trained carefully, prior to the arrival of the computer, in pricing a new private line circuit for a customer. Along came the computer with its pre-programming, and the job became simple: Punch in a few facts and figures, and "There's the answer in the window, dummy. Just copy it down. Try to do it right, please."

When the computer became available, the supervisors quickly realized that something had to be done to prevent resignations, boredom, indifference. A major step in the restructuring was to give the clerks the problem of pricing services within one or two industries and to work with certain men or women in the sales department. In other words, mini-groups were formed. Afterwards, one questionnaire response contained the freely written comment, "Thank God for my computer." A computer can de-skill, or it can become an employee's faithful servant.

Reason 11: The Industry Is Dying

I suspect that nothing much can be done to make good jobs for the mass of railroad employees; the industry is dying. Nor would I want to be an employee of an ice house, of a linseed oil manufacturer, or of a street railway, or a sailor in the American merchant marine. The telegram business is all but finished; without a new product line, the employees will soon be uncertain of their jobs, and the company uncertain of its very existence.

A company has to be quick on its feet to avoid death, but it can be done. A news item about slide rules says: "If you own a $40, Cadillac-class, mahogany model slide rule, one that made Keuffel and Esser a byword, you should hang on to it: It's becoming a collector's item. The electronic calculator wiped out the slide rule. The last engine-dividing machine, used by K & E to set the markings on the logarithmic rules, is in the Smithsonian Institution." Keuffel and Esser, to their credit, has become the distributors of Texas Instruments' line of calculators.

Some jobs die because the industry dies, obviously. The job redesigns cited in this book will not be very helpful in the case of dying industries. But this accounts for only a small number of dying jobs.

An Observation and Some Predictions

The main reason that jobs die, in my observation, is fragmentation of work, of responsibility. For when a person does only a fragment of what could be a reasonably complete piece of work, he or she loses control of the work and becomes unnecessarily dependent upon others. The writing of tight job specifications and the institution of perfect practices to be followed after the employees have been "perfectly trained" are more likely to be the results of job fragmentation than the cause.

In fact, I would go so far as to say that all 11 causes of job death discussed in this chapter are related aspects of the same basic disease—removal of responsibility. Some of them, such as instant rules, arise in an attempt to off-set troubles that were precipitated elsewhere. Consider again the truck driver whose van was smashed into by the drunk driver. The trucker had had hours of perfect training and had been put through hours of perfect practices. He was a master of defensive driving. His responsibility is clear enough: Drive that van to your work locations all day in such a way that you have no accidents. In 11 years, he had had none. But now that he has had his first accident, an instant rule will help him solve his problem, the boss thinks: "No left turns in front of this garage after four-fifteen P.M."

These observations on what causes jobs to die should alert the manager to any possible negative consequences (at least as seen by employees) of changes that are being proposed for the workplace. To take an example, a news story in *The New York Times** some years ago announced that optical scanners for supermarket checkout counters would lead to substantial savings of time and money. Each package label includes a vertical-line code such as this one:

*"Revolution Near at Checkout Counter," *The New York Times*, May 21, 1973.

This code is "read" by the optical scanner, and the electronic cash register does the rest. "The computer applies the proper price and rings it up on the cash register," the article states. "All this takes a fraction of a second. While guiding items across the scanner with one hand, the checker bags the customer's purchase with the other."

Perhaps all is well. But I suspect that this new approach to their job may be viewed as de-skilling by the checkers and be resisted one way or another. I would want to check it out very carefully indeed before making a commitment to investing in the new procedure. If the new equipment has merit but employees view it as de-skilling, how can their feelings be offset? For if it is not offset, the job of the checker dies a little.

3

---

the model for
work motivation

I FEEL MORE CONFIDENT in talking to the bosses about the problem of employee motivation since I reported on a study of a problem job at the headquarters of a company where I once worked. Parts of the report were not too complimentary, yet there sat the chairman of the board, quite attentive. The job under discussion was that of managers who were removed from the field, rotated into headquarters for a two-year assignment, and then returned to the field, where they were reassigned. Only people with excellent potential were rotated, as a rule. The very brightest. Some liked the trip to headquarters, but too many did not. That was the problem: Why not?

A quotation from an interview with a man who had returned to the field follows: "I could hardly wait to get back here to God's country. What happened at headquarters was this—and I watched other men and women go through it too. You spent the first six months of your assignment there straightening things out with Alcatraz Van Lines and getting your family settled; then six months learning the job, six months doing it, and the last six months calling back home nervously to learn what your next assignment was likely to be."

The tension lessened appreciably when the chairman

smiled and remarked, "He certainly 'told it like it was' when I was here on rotation, myself, some years ago. We would often make plans or decisions that were not implemented until we were rotated back home. We never had to live with our sins. Our replacement at headquarters did that. What can we do about this situation?"

Discussion led to the following policy, which vastly improved rotational practice. As far as possible, people on rotation were assigned to new projects, special projects, rather than to ongoing jobs. An assignment began and ended with the project, lasting not less than a year or two, but running perhaps four or five. Under this plan, people could get a very good sense of what it is like to work at headquarters while accomplishing a whole piece of work, something distinctive, something to talk about and interpret when they got back home. "We weren't at headquarters merely to hold someone's coat; we did the fighting ourselves," said a man who had rotated under this plan. Very often under the previous rotational plan, men and women were shunted into sideline jobs, somewhat in the role of observers, where they could not "mess up my smoothly running operation," as a boss said.

Consider this example in which the monthly product is a letter of advice on tax legislation, court decisions, or Internal Revenue Service rulings that affect a business or industry. The boss had four rotational assistants, all very bright, all college graduates, and all quite new to tax work or to writing a monthly letter. Under the two-year assignment rule, the boss used them purely as assistants. He signed all the letters himself and affixed his telephone number in case there were follow-up calls from field people. The assistant's job was greatly disliked by most—not all—who had held it. Yes, they would say, they had learned a lot, and, yes, they were glad to be back home. No, they did not want to go back on another rotational assignment to headquarters.

Under a revised job design, each assistant worked with the boss on one or two monthly letters, which went out with the boss's signature. Then the assistants were assigned, well in advance, three or four topics that would likely, but not surely, lead to letters. If the topics became newsworthy, the assistants issued the letter under their own names, complete with telephone number, and they became the current authority on the matter at hand. The boss complained laughingly one day, "I find that *I* am now the assistant." Under this plan the rotational assignment ended only when the boss, the manager-assistant, and the field organization jointly felt that a new assignment would advance the person's career. Clearly, one could succeed or fail under this plan, which, unlike mere rotation at the end of 24 months, is a very motivating situation.

Perhaps this is rather an obvious way to increase the motivational quality of a job. Nevertheless I humbly offer other obvious examples and some obvious observations about work motivation in this chapter. Don't be surprised to find in these next pages a dim view of many current strategies for increasing work motivation.

Some Approaches to Work Motivation

Before we consider the work model proposed in this book, let's look briefly at some other attempts to motivate employees. We have tried endlessly to improve the quality of products, to increase productivity, to do a good service through such expedients as:

—Coercion, threats, selected firing upon occasion.
—"Seduction," increased pay levels, building pay ladders guaranteed to motivate, running campaigns with prizes for winners, installing profit-sharing plans, and a hundred other economic ways. Always the question remains: What do we do for an encore before we go broke?
—Increased benefit programs, merely a variation of straight pay, for they can be priced out also. Same problem.
—Improved communication. This route to improving

productivity became a smash hit after World War II. But we still have productivity problems in corporations with excellent communication programs. The obstinate employee is not listening, apparently.

—Improved human relations, another smash hit; attitude surveys (my earliest corporate assignment, in fact); improved management training on human needs, aimed in essence at producing a peaceable kingdom, one where the animals could work in harmony or at least tolerate each other.

—Improved work environment, layouts, acoustic silencing, planters, dividers, air conditioning, color coordination, lounges, decorator toilets.

Now we offer you job design and work organization as a way of motivating people. Perhaps it is just another panacea. I think not, but time will tell. The problem the chairman in our example above saw with rotational assignments had existed years earlier, but he did not recognize it as a problem until someone called it to his attention. The obvious solution was to change the work assignment to one that began and ended with a whole piece of work. Surely that does not come under the heading of "personnel panacea." This is not a trick program aimed at motivating "them," out there on the floor. This is an effort to share knowledge at the managerial level as to what kind of work motivates all by itself.

Work Itself as a Motivator

In the long run the work itself must be the motivator. Otherwise the motivation involved is the motivation to acquire money, leisure, friendship, or security. Too often we use wages, benefits, improved communication, or the promise of human decency in supervisor–employee relations as a "buy-off," a kind of bribe, for productivity. Those facets of the job should be adequate in their own right. People deserve to be treated decently.

Now let us talk strictly about *work* motivation. People learn early in life that work is the avenue to food, clothing, shelter, security, human worth and dignity, self-fulfillment. A national tragedy exists when young people have no chance to perform useful work, for then they cannot learn that work itself, making a useful product, giving a useful service, can be rewarding, too, just as is money. Human motivation, broadly speaking, is the attraction or repulsion one feels for doing a million things, from eating anchovies to listening to zither music. Most motivation is acquired behavior, not innate. Work motivation is a good example of an acquired attraction or repulsion for doing something.

Most employees, especially the young, come to companies voluntarily to earn money for food, shelter, etc. They frequently know little about the work that is available, what it's like to be a programmer, a salesperson, a service representative. Their motivation is primarily to meet life's basic needs.

As psychologist Abraham Maslow and others have pointed out, when a human need is met, it is no longer a motivator. The human animal then goes on to meet other needs. Work can be a marvelous motivator because it permits us to meet needs other than sheer economic ones, needs such as friendship, a chance to show what we can do, a chance to be in on excitement, an opportunity to feel needed. Tending a telephone switchboard or repairing telephones can be tiresome. But watch what happens when a city like New York has a brownout, a flood, or a fire in which a huge central telephone office building is burned out, as happened there several years ago. The building was so large that it could have handled all the telephones for Rochester, New York. In all these instances employees who were off work started streaming voluntarily into other buildings where they knew they would be needed.

Voluntarily? Recall the earlier instance when the boss said, "Lord, give us a snowstorm!" A cynic may argue, "They know they'll get paid." Yes, they will. A makeshift record system for payroll will spring up also. For a successful corporation to ask people to work for nothing would be indecent behavior. But the truth was that people came back to work because, "Well, I know I'm needed," or "I knew that the switchboard would be lit up like a Christmas tree." Work motivation, an internalized willingness and desire to work, is as simple as that: I'm needed, this product is needed, this service is needed. This is learned behavior. Do your employees have a chance to learn it? To overlearn it, the way we overlearn the skill of reading, so that we never wonder about how to read, we just read? Is one likely to learn this if the job is some tiny fragment of work that anyone could do? Or does the job call for skilled and needed people who will want to provide their services? A profound truth that is often overlooked is simply this: Work itself *can* be a motivator.

The Model for Maximum Job Motivation

At the heart of helping people to become motivated is this general but simple model:

—Let the employees know what the organization's objectives are. Communicate with them about the particular business and objectives of their segment, the particular jobs and goals in their organization.
—Let them know how their business or organizational segment is performing with respect to purpose and objectives.
—Start them on some part of the segment, some piece of the total work, a reasonable module, a "slice of the business."
—Let them have maximum control over what they do. Give them the power to act, increasing control or power as they learn and earn the right to it. Make this an explicit step; tell them that's the way the job is designed.
—Let them do as much of the job of fulfilling the purpose

of the business segment as they can; expand the job as they expand their ability (no rigid job specs, please).
—If helpful, organize self-contained work units, or mini-groups, of mutually supporting workers, so that a final product or service emerges from the group. (Some jobs cannot be improved except by inclusion in a larger grouping of jobs.)
—Give employees lots of feedback as to how they are doing.
—Give them access to staff support for information and expertise so that they can perform more effectively within their own segment (e.g., the industrial engineer, cost accountant, methods and practices people, computer experts).
—Give them access to the boss for knowledge and support also.

There is very little more to be said about what's at the heart of the matter, the human psychology of the situation. But now that we've said it, how do we do it, how do we put our words into action?

Translating the Model into Jobs

Now we must call upon managers, industrial engineers, equipment designers, anyone who has a finger in the job pie, and ask for their diagnostic help and understanding as we translate the model into good jobs.* There are four aspects to be considered, regardless of whether we are reexamining an existing job or laying out a new work flow prior to slicing it into jobs.

THE MODULE OF WORK
The first consideration is the *module* of work someone is to perform. The questions we must answer are these:

*My particular thanks go to my former colleague, Malcolm B. Gillette, Director, Human Performance Systems, AT&T, New York City, and his current staff for some of the ideas in this reformulation of an earlier model.

Where does the work begin and end as a whole? What is the product or service? Can one person perform the whole task? Can employees acquire and maintain the necessary knowledge and skill for the task? Will they be able to meet reasonable, objective performance standards, for we are going to have them? Will they be able to meet the equally important, nonobjective standards, such as maintaining good product appearance or maintaining a gracious manner and desirable appearance in dealing with customers?

Although the work may flow through half a dozen steps or stages, the employee must have as functionally complete a module as possible. If six steps are involved, half a dozen people could be lined up, each to perform one-sixth of the work before passing it on to the next person. All this would be done in the name of efficiency, so that training time will be minimized, and workers can develop great skill, the ability to knock the work out very fast. More likely, what they will develop is great boredom and great indifference.

Evidence is now reasonably strong that such a six-step arrangement will create at least these problems: Work may have to be logged in and out in an effort to keep track of its progress, thus creating more jobs. A coordinator may have to be appointed. Since no one person is responsible for the work or service from beginning to end, except the boss, the number of errors will surely rise, leading to the need for quality control jobs. Approximately the first 20 percent of the time spent at each stage after the first will be on checking out the situation as received. This front-end load of work can be eliminated each time we figure out a way of letting the same person who performed the first step perform the next step, and the next after that, right up to some limit of practicality. And if one person can perform all six steps, then we free a coordinator and have reduced or eliminated the need for logging work and for extra quality control. *Functional completeness* is a marvelous goal in design jobs; in this case the work becomes the job. We may have to settle for far less, but we must minimize the number of jobs in the lineup, and we must make each slice as meaningful as possible.

CONSISTENCY IN THE WORK SITUATION

Now that the work flow and the least number of jobs or slices across that work flow have been determined, more questions must be asked. How can we make this a *consistent situation* for the worker?

Can the worker forecast the load, the work volume that will hit? How about deadlines—can they be set meaningfully, not arbitrarily? Can we set the work input so that a worker gets it consistently from a certain group of customers or clients? Can the worker have an area, a piece of "turf"? Must this worker provide a special technology consistently? Can it be made interesting and challenging?

If a worker has a functionally complete module of work, and if it comes from a certain place and goes out to a certain place consistently, we are well on our way toward building a very good job.

CONTROL

The third important ingredient is *power to act,* or *control.* If the worker is going to be held responsible for the product or service, and that is one of our goals, can he or she take action if something starts to go wrong?

What can we let workers do, on their own, on this job? Can they schedule the work, in and out, to meet the deadlines, for example? Can they make estimates and requests for parts, supplies, inventory, or must this be done by the boss? What if workers feel that too much stock is lying around, in the way? If time requirements, deadlines, costs, budgets, qualities, and quantities are being met, can employees work on their own? Can employees call for help, scrounge, get it any way they can, if deadline problems or other problems loom ahead? Can workers go directly to workers at previous stages if problems are emerging, or must they go to the boss, who will go to another boss, to resolve the problem? If someone above actually needs to know what progress is being made, can a Xerox copy of the information be sent to that person while the work goes right ahead, without waiting for consent? Can workers be given small budgets for their jobs, or the right to ask for services directly within certain boundaries, so that work can go right ahead or start faster after a problem occurs?

FEEDBACK

The fourth and final ingredient is useful *feedback* from the work, an ingredient that is only too frequently missing.

Where, or what, is the feedback? Do employees know themselves when things are going wrong, or have we mistakenly set it up so that employees find out from the supervisor rather than from a dial, a red light, a printout, an irate customer/client? Is the feedback as fast and direct as we can possibly make it? Is it individualized, the employee's own feedback, or is it merely the average for a group—a form of feedback that is second best. (As an example, offer to keep score for four golfers. At the end of the round, tell them you have only their average score to offer.) Is the feedback work-related, or is it secondary (failure to be cooperative, to give to the United Fund, to park properly in the employee lot, etc.)? Is it consistent? Are other employees measured in the same way? Is it reliable information?

The concept of feedback is borrowed from electrical engineering, where means are set up so that a mechanism senses when it is beginning to malfunction and can take steps internally to reduce the error back toward some zero point. If my analogy is way off, I hope electrical engineers will forgive me. The point is that the work situation should be self-adjusting rather than boss-adjusting. We've had the latter quite long enough. When employees are asked, "How do you know whether or not you are doing a good job?" they very frequently answer: "I don't know, actually, how well I'm doing," or "No news is good news," or "Did I get the work out on time?" The third of these replies is the only desirable one, and it doesn't go far enough. How about the quality, for example?

Employees have every right to have a copy of the checklist used by the boss when he or she evaluates performance, to know how they are being judged. As Odiorne, exponent of Management by Objectives, has wisely pointed out, it isn't cheating to know how the boss is judging you. An ideal feedback arrangement goes well beyond that. Ideally, the employee should be able to tell the boss how well he or she, the employee, is doing, for the employee has exactly the same information as the boss, and the employee has it earlier.

So much for the model, the ingredients that make for a good job: a functionally complete module, work in a consistent situation, with reasonable and necessary power to act and keep things under control, plus plenty of feedback. Some writers add "variety" to the requirements. As I see it, jobs designed with these four ingredients will tend to be quite varied, the very opposite of monotonous. I would not add items to a job merely for purposes of variety; the items should belong to the job naturally.

We need not concern ourselves here with the question, Will this job engage a person's attention forever? It probably won't. Later chapters of this book go into this issue: the problem of self-renewal.

This prescription for a good job, calling for four ingredients, assumes that two other important requirements will be met—but they are not part of the job. First, we assume that the training department will be able to cooperate, to supply the necessary knowledge and skill—but no more than that—so that the employee can get started. No useless knowledge, no "cold storage" training should occur in this ideal training effort. Just get the beginners started, and supply only what the work situation itself cannot supply in an efficient and timely way. If the training jobs are built properly, their feedback will answer the question: "Did my trainees succeed when they went onto the job?" We can think of training as the front end of the job.

And there is a back end, too: Does the whole work environment support the workers in their effort to be useful? Do practices and procedures sustain them? Are the measurement plan and the standards just right? How about light, heat, ventilation, the cafeteria, and the other factors in the surrounding environment, do they sustain or annoy? Pay plans, holidays, benefits, and similar items, do they also sustain the employees in their feeling that this is not only a reasonably good job, but it's a good organization to work for?

Lethal Information Loops: A Violation of the Model

Managers cannot escape having a model for laying out work and job assignments. They have to believe *something* about how to get work done. It is easy to accept the model offered here while retaining parts of an older model, and the two may be in open conflict. The following example is intended to help managers make a decision as to which way to go.

Now that computer printouts are so readily available, and in an effort to stay on top of their jobs, the top bosses may easily make the mistake of asking to see the results of a work unit's operations before the members of the unit themselves see it. This may happen accidentally, simply because the boss is located at headquarters, near the computer, and the work unit is out in the field, where reports arrive a day or two later. This situation is lethal in the sense that the field people learn to worry about the report in the interim between its coming off the computer and their seeing it. If it's bad, they may get a stormy call from the big boss while lacking the information the boss has.

These anxieties can lead not only to poor performance but to self-defeating efforts. In a situation I observed, the general manager chided a division manager reporting to him, in an open meeting, about April's poor showing for the division. The division manager said he was indeed sorry and had already taken steps to correct the situation.

"How could you?" asked the general manager. "You haven't seen the report. It just came to my desk this morning, and I didn't even bring it along to this meeting."

The division manager, a bold fellow indeed, said, "Look, you've caught me before when I didn't know what the computer would show. So I have a few clerks hand-tally the figures on the last day of the month, which enables me to take action before you holler at me!"

And a district manager who was sitting there spoke up to his boss, the division manager, "That's interesting. Believe it or not, I do the same thing for my district to avoid your yelling at me without my knowing the facts! I have a clerk hand-tally my figures also."

The problem is that the computerized information system is running in the wrong direction. The district bosses (lowest level) should see their results first, the division bosses (next higher level) should see them second, with the general manager seeing results for all the units last. Such a feedback loop would enable the junior bosses to take corrective steps right away, and it would save half a dozen clerical staff/days, the very reason a computer was involved in the first place. As indicated in the next section, not only will employees avoid negative feedback if they can, but they won't perform as well under a system in which such feedback is feared as they will under a system of positive reinforcement.

Positive Reinforcement for Good Performance

Learn to reinforce good performance positively. In the last 20 years, dramatic advances have been made by behavioral scientists in demonstrating the vast superiority of using positive reinforcement to strengthen desired behavior over using punishment to eliminate undesirable behavior. In working with animals, all experimenters have to do is time a food reward properly with an accidental movement in the direction they desire the animal to take, and after a number of trials the animal will move that way repeatedly. The experimenters don't even have to reward the animal every time in order to elicit the desired behavior repeatedly. The threat of punishment can be used, but it is not nearly as successful a motivator as is a reward. I wouldn't try withholding any paychecks from any employees of mine if I valued my safety; that isn't likely to act as a motivator to anything but anger and looking for a new job. But we do need to examine the way we use the reinforcement available to us every day as bosses.

Money as the reinforcer is the basis of incentive systems used so frequently in manufacturing, and hated so often by labor unions. The complaint is often made that *control* is really not with the workers; that's why they can't make out well financially with these incentive systems. And as soon as productivity drops for whatever reason, the cut in money becomes very punishing indeed. Money is a poor motivator for many jobs. Use it if you can, but don't be too hopeful. In the meantime, let's look at other reinforcers of good performance.

The service that was performed so well as to lead a customer to say to an employee, "Thank you very much," has been nicely reinforced. Design a job so that employees can earn reinforcement every day, or almost every day. (Remember, also, that a "customer" might be someone inside the organization; we usually call them "clients" in this case.)

If possible, arrange the job situation so that employees can get reinforcement from their peers. A mini-group is more likely to provide this for its members than a job situation where employees work for themselves. Work in a mini-group leads to remarks such as, "Thanks for the assist, Joe; much appreciated." A real motivator for many people, say psychologists, is the need to be with and work with other people; thus jobs can meet social as well as basic economic needs. The mini-group should be assembled carefully (not all people want to be part of a group), and it must have goals, work measurements, and work standards, which will set the stage for this source of valuable reinforcement.

We mustn't forget that another valuable source of reinforcement is one's own judgment of an act. Experienced golfers do not need to have the club pro or friends tell them when they have made a great shot down the middle of the fairway or out of the rough. They appraise and praise their own performance. A good job design is one where, with experience, the worker knows, "That was well done."

One day I walked up behind a wireman in a silent, new, central office that Western Electric was building. He was running continuity and adequacy checks on a part of a mainframe, so intently that I walked on tiptoe and waited to speak. Suddenly his whole face lit up and he said aloud, "Hot damn!" That's self-reinforcement. It's the essence of craftsmanship. Every well-designed job should have meters, measures, reports, or some way of letting you know when to say, "Hot damn!" Countless jobs do not.

If your own employees are competent to judge, they can supply reinforcement to themselves, to each other, and to you. It's very nice to hear one of them say at the end of a tough conference you led, "That was a nice job, boss."

In summary, reinforcement in the work situation can come from any of these sources: oneself; the boss; customers/clients; peers and other workers; subordinates.

In too many cases, the boss has been the only source of reinforcement. Jobs need to be set up in such a way that the employee can get reinforcement from all or at least some of the other sources.

Consider, instead, how we tend to reinforce employees. We storm at poor work and ignore good work. We say nothing about a job well done, on the grounds that "That's what we're paying them for!" We find ways of introducing a little of the "fear of God" into them when most employees know only too well what would happen if they lost their job. They don't need to have additional reminders in the form of threats of punishment.

Sometimes we miss opportunities to give positive reinforcement. I recall a case where at 5:15 P.M., a woman heard her phone ringing persistently behind the just-locked door to the little, three-person office of a struggling new business. As she hurriedly unlocked the door, went back in, and answered the phone, she heard her boss, who waited outside, say, "Look, no heroics. Let's go home, please." He could have said "Thank you, Jane." Another woman related an instance to me where a business luncheon involved a martini lunch, and then coffee. During coffee she said, "I want to go back to the office. I've got some phone calls to make." Her boss said, "What's the hurry? Let's have a liqueur." Another missed opportunity. The reply should have been, "Thank you, that's very thoughtful."

Managers who want to use modern learning theory must learn to teach new employees the job, reinforcing them for each and any aspect of good performance until the employees can do the whole job correctly almost every time. If they make a mistake, the boss should help them get back on the right track, reinforcing them for the part of the work they have done well. Reinforce the employees if the job succeeds, show somehow that you know and care. It may be difficult, but managers must deny themselves the acknowledged luxury of giving other people hell.

People who have been beaten down by the boss are still there, with their faces often covered by a "mask" as in an ancient theatrical play. The smile is there, but not the motivation to work. One of my closest friends in Bell Canada once replied, when I was pointing out an unnecessarily high rate of force loss, "I hear what you say, Bob, about high rates of force loss, but what really bothers me is the great number of people we've lost who are still with us." These are the people who can't leave for any of a dozen reasons, such as: no other skills, family problems, personal illness, or nearness of retirement. They can be brought to life again in many cases through repotting. Get them in a new, good job situation, a job designed along the lines of the concepts presented in this book. Then reinforce them properly. Don't be content to let such people make safe plays, like a football team that is ahead and is merely " running out the clock."

A Common-Sense Verification

There is a great need for managers to take a different view of jobs and the question of motivation. The national situation is not getting better. In *Work Is Here to Stay, Alas,* Levitan and Johnston say that the situation is virtually hopeless. Work is work, and not much can be done about it. They say, "The evolution of the post-industrial economy has clearly not resulted in a quality of work revolution. Not surprisingly, high differences in jobs remain."* Closely examined, neither the white-collar jobs nor the stereotype service jobs of the post-industrial economy indicate the rebirth of humanized work. I agree, but I am not so pessimistic about the future as they are, or I would not have written this book. We can do something about job quality.

And what shall we say about employees? Are they really willing to work hard, as Douglas McGregor implied in his Theory Y?† Or are they a bunch of goof-offs, as claimed by other theories, which McGregor collectively labeled Theory X? I would propose this view: Most of us have to work. We are not independently wealthy. Very few of us can get by with charity, or are satisfied to get by with it. Perhaps some of us work because we subscribe to the Protestant Ethic, that is, we *must* work at something, and work hard, or we feel we are bad people.

*S. A. Levitan and W. B. Johnston, *Work Is Here to Stay, Alas.* Salt Lake City: Olympus, 1973, p. 109.

†D. McGregor, *Human Side of Enterprise.* New York: McGraw-Hill, 1960

Many people work—as volunteers—in order to fill their time meaningfully. Little or no money is involved. If we were to withdraw from their jobs all the people who work as volunteers, many of our communities and towns would screech to a halt. Almost every hospital has many, many people working in it for nothing; school boards frequently work for nothing, as do town councils, volunteer fire departments, police auxiliary units, town zoning commissions, emergency squads—there is a long list of jobs filled by volunteers. Why is this so?

Indeed, the motivation can be quite complex. It may be a mixture of the need to achieve, the need for power, and the need to affiliate with other people.* At this time, we need not pursue the theories of human behavior or motivation much further than to say this: People's attitudes toward work, their motivation to work, are not inherent, they are learned behaviors.

What the individual learns about work has its roots in the family situation and the schools. But an even greater influence on the attitudes that young men and women will have toward work for the rest of their lives is their experience in their first job—whether in a business, government organization, hospital, school system, or anywhere else. The attitudes that they form here—whether sour or favorable—will often stay with them until the very end of their work career.

In concluding this chapter, I am urging this point of view. *Let us lay out the work situation so that work will appeal to the more highly educated young people who are with us today.* If we learn to look at jobs the right way, if we learn how to design, to redesign, and to organize them, we will find that most jobs can be improved. Quite a few of them can be improved a great deal. Only a very few cannot be improved at all, and even here a strategy remains: Include such a job in a mini-group, a set of meaningful, related jobs.

This model applies to jobs at all levels in an organiza-

*D. McClelland, in J. W. Atkinson (ed.), *Motives in Fantasy, Action, and Society.* New York: Van Nostrand Reinhold, 1958.

tion. Peter F. Drucker points especially to the problem emerging at the management level, where so much recruiting is done directly from colleges. Because of the mid-50's "baby boom," many highly educated young people are now at the employment doorstep when the opportunity for advancement will be slow indeed. The promise of early promotion used so much in recent years is not possible; the organizational chart is already filled with competent people who are only slightly older. Drucker concludes that we will have to learn how to restructure jobs for the young:

> In the last twenty years we have tended to make entrance jobs smaller and smaller and less demanding; we had to get young people ready for promotions fast. Now we will have to structure jobs on the assumption that even a capable and hard-working person may have to spend many years on or near the entrance level. Early assignments will have to be made more demanding and more challenging; the ambitious young person must have an opportunity to achieve—or to fail.[†]

If we have work that needs to be accomplished and we are willing to pay for it, we must set the stage so that we can say, as Maslow might say, "Here is a way of meeting your needs—food, shelter, clothing. Here is a way of finding security. Here is a way of meeting your social needs, and your needs for self-esteem. If you are a good worker, you can actualize your whole life."

Our problem is a very practical one: We must set the stage so that more, rather than fewer, people can find *real* meaning in their work. If we examine our own needs for a meaningful, consistent module of work, one that we can control, one with good feedback, we will undoubtedly concede that there is common-sense verification of the work model presented here. If, in addition, we think about the behavior of the many people who work for *nothing,* we can verify again that they are indeed working for *something.*

† *Wall Street Journal,* February 5, 1979.

Most of us do many small jobs for nothing. The jobs make sense, and meaningful work can be a powerful motivator. The fact that we pay people for work should not delude us into thinking that money is the only or the best motivator. Money is a *necessary* element for the accomplishment of many jobs, but, as a work motivator, it is an engine running on one cylinder.

4

---

what motivates?

PERHAPS IT IS EVIDENT that certain strategies are better than others for improving or increasing the motivational quality of a job. In this chapter I attempt to discriminate among some of these strategies and to select the ones more likely to win. I have labeled these "principles." Although one is on safer ground to merely present some general observations, with the admonition, "Keep all these points of view in mind; select the one that will work best in your situation," I will boldly select the better strategy for the manager who wants to maximize the motivational quality of task assignment. I am particularly eager to have industrial engineers and equipment designers consider these ideas, for in the near future engineers will be the key people determining the quality of work for millions of people.

Job Design Strategies

PRINCIPLE 1: Tasks that challenge without overwhelming or underestimating the person will tend to be the most motivating.

DISCUSSION: In scores of work situations, workers have simply stopped when production lines got too fast. On the other hand, they have become indifferent and inattentive when the pace of work was too slow. All aspects of a job, not merely speed of work, are subject to the same principle. A job should be enlarged to the point where many employees will feel it is a meaningful "slice" or module, a complete phase of some sort. Mere job enlargement aimed at giving variety is less valuable than including only those steps that make a logical whole, but that might or might not contain variety.

A derivative of this principle is: Job enrichment is better than job enlargement, and both are far better than job fragmentation or task simplification (reduction) as a source of work motivation. A smaller module is not as good as a larger module, provided the module is not so large as to overwhelm individuals. The tendency in task design, unfortunately, is to "underwhelm" employees, especially where parts of the whole job have been automated.

STRATEGY: *In designing jobs, aim for a middle range— neither too difficult nor too easy for most people. If possible, tailor jobs to individuals, increasing responsibilities as the individual grows.*

PRINCIPLE 2: Both job enrichment and job enlargement are more motivating than job rotation.

DISCUSSION: Simple rotation—moving workers from job to job each day or each week—has some motivational effect and produces some economies, but studies at the Philips Corporation in the Netherlands* also indicate that many employees dislike any further rotation when they get to a job that is better than the others they have experienced before. Job rotation may indeed help the manager by creating a more flexible and versatile workforce and by making mutual assistance possible. It is down-rated here as compared to job enrichment (giving workers functionally complete, consistent modules with feedback and con-

*Work Structuring: A Summary of Projects at Philips. Netherlands: N.V. Philips Gloeilampenfabrieken, 1970.

trol). Job rotation does not change any of the specific jobs through which employees are rotated. Job enlargement (giving workers two or three tasks to perform rather than one) is intermediate in effect. All three are attempts to improve existing jobs. Job redesign may go beyond this.

STRATEGY: *In job redesign aim at least for job enrichment; don't stop with halfway measures such as job rotation or enlargement. And be prepared to go all the way to a reconsideration of a whole work flow.*

PRINCIPLE 3: The chances for employees to become involved in their work are greater if control of the work (power to act, responsibility, authority) is moved downward to the employees rather than upward to the boss.

DISCUSSION: In a sense, the success of this principle depends upon the previous ones. If a whole cycle of work cannot be laid out for individuals, like total responsibility for producing a telephone directory, the big items of control cannot be delegated by the supervisor to employees as readily. When tasks are distributed among people, it is natural for a boss to retain control in order to coordinate the work.

STRATEGY: *Give the boss so many people and design the jobs so well that the boss will be glad to pass along control of the work as individuals prove their competence.*

PRINCIPLE 4: If the module and its control have been set for some time, it is easier to reassign and improve control than to restructure the module.

DISCUSSION: Changes in the control of work—the power to decide what to do in this or that situation—are sometimes more appropriate and easier to effect than are changes in the module. Usually the boss merely has to give up control. Almost all efforts at job enrichment can result in improvement of worker control. On the other hand, the basic module of work may be harder to change because it is fragmented between different bosses or departments. Often the module may be reasonably good already. Examples from our studies are the jobs of the service representative and the telephone installer, both of which were basically good assignments already. Improvements were made in control and feedback, however.

STRATEGY: *At the outset of a job redesign effort, examine the possible gains to be had from restructuring control, before tearing up production lines or reorganizing departments and people.*

PRINCIPLE 5: Feedback (information about success/failure) from an aspect of the work itself (customer/client/task) is a far better reinforcer of good performance than is indirect feedback through a superior.

DISCUSSION: During the learning period, feedback from the supervisor (or other trainer) is important. Once the employee has started to do productive work, direct feedback from the work is better, for two reasons. First, employees will receive feedback more frequently if customers/clients/tasks are in the loop. Second, employees have a chance to straighten out problems before the boss learns about them. When the employee hears from the boss eventually, the chances for positive rather than negative feedback are greater.

STRATEGY: *Bosses should gradually phase themselves out as sources of feedback about employees' work, but not completely out, since in the end they are accountable.*

PRINCIPLE 6: If a work module has been well designed and control over it has been vested in the employee, desirable, helpful feedback is easier to obtain than if the module is poorly designed or control over it is in the wrong hands.

DISCUSSION: When responsibility for a task is divided, feedback must also be divided, and thus it is less individualized and effective. If the module and control are correctly assigned, however, the responsible person is the natural receiver of any feedback. When individual clerks were given the job of compiling entire telephone directories, there was no question as to who was responsible for an error in compilation, or who should get the credit when directories turned out to be entirely error-free.

STRATEGY: *Design jobs so that the immediately responsible employee is the first to learn about a disaster in his or her module. Train bosses to say nothing if the item is corrected. On the other hand, bosses should reinforce the employee who has received a good response from customer/ client/task.*

PRINCIPLE 7: Individuals with complementary specialties serving in mutually supportive and responsible teams (mini-groups) result in a more highly motivated workforce than when pools of similar specialists attempt to support other pools of different specialists.

DISCUSSION: This is true because the mini-group provides feedback that it can act upon much faster. We were especially impressed by the Ferguson (Missouri) Telephone District example, as reported in the *Harvard Business Review* (January-February 1973). The service representatives, clerks, and cathode ray operator-typists were arranged in an ellipse. When a service representative and a clerk had completed the paperwork for a new telephone, for example, they could simply hand the order to the CRT operator-typist sitting in the center of the ellipse, who typed the information directly into a computer for storage. Changes in the order or the record could be handled just as fast and easily because of the direct interaction among the employees. Previously, orders had to travel from the representatives to their supervisors, then to the supervisor of the service-order-records unit, and finally to the CRT operator-typists, with a confirmation copy of the computer-stored record making its way back along the same route.

The new physical arrangement was undoubtedly a success factor in this case, but the resulting psychological interdependence was the real key to the remarkable improvement in work performance. A similar setup involving computer input terminals had been used somewhat earlier in the treasury department of AT&T. Referred to as *mini-groups* by Assistant Treasurer A. P. Luse and his staff, the concept proved to be a highly efficient way to handle the records of stockholders or bond owners.

STRATEGY: *Set up mini-groups of complementary workers rather than units of homogeneous workers. If physically possible, arrange their workplaces in ellipses, circles, or squared-off areas so that workers can see the progress of jobs and quickly help each other when bottlenecks occur or when someone needs relief.*

PRINCIPLE 8: An isolated job that has proved difficult to enrich will become a more desirable, productive job if the worker is included in a relevant mini-group.

DISCUSSION: Because of their isolated location, the operators of the new cathode ray input tubes in the Ferguson Telephone District example mentioned above were a problem unit until they were dispersed, along with supporting clerks, among the service representatives whose work they typed. Their two supervisors were reassigned also, resulting in better use of labor.

STRATEGY: *Don't give up on redesigning any troublesome work situation. If a job can't be changed much (because it calls for the operation of a console or keyboard, for example), consider placing it in a mini-group.*

PRINCIPLE 9: Members of a mini-group (workers with different but related jobs) will learn each other's jobs, support each other in crisis, and require less down-time for training than will units or sections whose members all do the same kind of work.

DISCUSSION: If there are several jobs and pay levels in

a mini-group, those on the lower levels, usually the newer employees, have a good opportunity to watch more highly paid workers, to judge whether they can do the higher-level jobs, and to aspire realistically to these higher-level jobs. Training time for the upward-oriented mini-group member is only a fraction of that required for a novice who has never seen the job performed. The new mini-group member may or may not want some of the higher-level jobs; this is a good way to find out.

STRATEGY: *Don't hesitate to have different jobs and pay levels in a mini-group. Design procedures to be flexible enough that a person can try his or her skill at a tougher job without upsetting other people.*

PRINCIPLE 10: Mini-groups with increased control and feedback will maintain good levels of service or productivity over longer periods than will groups of workers with identical jobs who depend on supervisors or others for work assignments, control, and feedback.

DISCUSSION: The assumption here is that the mini-group is formed with a realistic service or product as a base. Thus the mini-group will tend to sustain itself and operate without a supervisor or other staff support much better than will a unit of employees whose work is fed to it from other workers rather than from their own customer/client/task. The mini-group generates and completes its own work; it needs less outside help. Savings in supervisory costs are a striking feature of the mini-group design.

STRATEGY: *Don't set up too many supervisory jobs in designing a mini-group. Keep supervisory numbers and layers as lean as possible, even at the start, forcing the mini-group to take care of itself.*

Management Implications

PRINCIPLE 11: Employees are more likely to accept

added responsibility if appropriate feedback and control are included.

DISCUSSION: Interestingly enough, this is one of the
most debated points between many traditionalists and
those in the new job design effort. The small amount of
evidence we have from our own studies indicates that 50
to 85 percent of employees will accept additional responsibility if it is offered to them.* Some critics claim that further evidence will show that no more than 15 to 20 percent
will accept broader responsibility. Furthermore, they
claim that the job redesign effort is a waste of time even
for these 15 to 20 percent because people who want responsibility are soon to be in management or in other
better jobs anyhow. However, if we truly believe that employees are our most important resource, then no fraction
of that resource should be underutilized at any time or be
permitted to grow accustomed to inferior job designs
prior to moving into management.

STRATEGY: *Take a chance that added responsibility,
with feedback and control, will be accepted by employees in
such numbers as to make the total effort worthwhile.*

PRINCIPLE 12: A total job redesign effort that starts at
the bottom of an organization is easier
and more natural to effect than a job enrichment effort that starts at the top.

DISCUSSION: Bell System studies have indicated consistently that responsibility for work tends to creep upward
in the organization. If we start reorganizing work at too
high a level or at upper levels, we may be organizing work
into new forms that shouldn't be performed at that level
at all.

STRATEGY: *Start by redesigning the fundamental jobs
in the organization. In so doing, pieces of work, control
over work, or feedback from work that has crept to higher
levels in the organization can be placed back where they*

*R.N. Ford, *Motivation Through the Work Itself* (New York: AMACOM, 1969), pp.
126-127.

belong. The result will be employees who are better moti-
vated and functionally more capable.

PRINCIPLE 13: When a managerial job has become bur-
dened with tasks that belong on levels
below it, it may be necessary to fix the
managerial job first. This is likely to fix
the lower-level job automatically.

DISCUSSION: Clues to the likelihood that managerial
jobs need to be redesigned may be: managers voluntarily
taking demotions to their old jobs, managers threatening
to unionize, or statements such as, "I wish I had my tools
(or truck) back again," or "If it weren't for the money,
they could shove this job." If managers have these attitudes about their jobs, there is little chance that they will
work seriously and enthusiastically on the redesign or
improvement of the jobs below them; they will kill the
effort with apathy.

STRATEGY: *Should you find yourself in such a delaying*
game, involve managers and yourself in improving their
own jobs first. There is a high probability that they will
automatically improve jobs below their level by passing
down various items of module/control/feedback. Such a
strategy not only solves problems at two levels, but acts
simultaneously as an excellent practical course in man-
agement training and development.

PRINCIPLE 14: If the lower jobs in an organization are
improved, job improvement will natu-
rally move upward in the organization.

DISCUSSION: In the course of redesigning the jobs of
many different groups of middle management people
(third level), we have been struck by the statement made
repeatedly by their superiors (fourth or fifth level): "At
this moment we may not have done very much for our
third-level people, but I want to assure you that my job
has been enriched very much, indeed!" These were headquarters groups where management jobs at the third

level were, in fact, jobs basic to the success of headquarters' mission. Determining which jobs are basic may require hard analytical thinking. When those jobs are loaded as they should be, the boss can then take on work more suitable for the boss's level.

STRATEGY: *Identify basic jobs—that is, work that simply must be done—and make those the key jobs in the redesign effort. Be sure to involve some people from all the levels that might become involved in the long run, including such staff people as methods and procedures engineers, standards and results people, and labor relations staff, if not at the outset, then during the progress of the redesign effort. There are more people who need to be involved than only those who hold the basic job being redesigned.*

PRINCIPLE 15: Changes in work arrangements that start at the bottom are more likely to be effective than changes that start at the top.

DISCUSSION: Here we are assuming that individual jobs have already been improved and someone is now wondering how to put these jobs together into meaningful configurations or arrangements.

STRATEGY: *When an organization has been running poorly, resist the temptation to merely shift bosses or rearrange boxes on organizational charts, until after basic jobs have been reexamined and reorganized.*

Motivational Strength

PRINCIPLE 16: That job will motivate most which best meets the current needs of an employee.

DISCUSSION: In our society at this time we can easily see that these needs are: maintenance, security, fellowship, self-esteem, achievement, psychological growth, and self-actualization. We do not wish to imply that all of these needs are universal. Some populations have very low self-actualization needs, needs to grow and to learn. For vast masses of people who live in impoverished economic circumstances, the struggles for security and maintenance of life are primary. To talk to these people about job satisfaction and self-actualization would be sheer nonsense. Our jobs should be tailored to employees available to us. The motivational needs of people in many other countries, such as Sweden, Denmark, Norway, Holland, France, or Italy, are similar to those of Americans or Canadians. Great Britain and Ireland may be in-between cases, with Japan rapidly emerging as a country whose people have work needs similar to those of people in the major Western economies. Should our economy run into hard times, the need for well-designed jobs may recede as employees scramble to meet the basic needs of food, shelter, and clothing. But when the economy again improves, the other needs will resurface.

STRATEGY: *Design jobs to meet as many needs as possible. This should give one employer a competitive edge over another for acquiring and retaining talent, especially if the jobs of both meet the basic economic needs equally well. While good job design should not be expected to offset important economic gains that a prospective employee might receive by going elsewhere, it should help you retain talented people if economic considerations are about equal.*

PRINCIPLE 17: Employees working at highly motivating tasks will tend to work more willingly than those performing less motivating tasks.

DISCUSSION: The signs of unwillingness to work may appear as absenteeism or tardiness, especially before and after weekends or holidays. Employees working in jobs they don't like are quite susceptible to campaigns for shorter work weeks, gliding time (flexible hours), birthdays off with pay or other new paid holidays, and similar manifestations of the reaction, "Let me out of here!"

Attention directed primarily at the motivational quality of the work itself may solve these and other problems.

For example, it may be possible to work such items as gliding time and the four-day week into the control aspect of a good job. Consider this example: When almost all directory compilation clerks in California had their own directories, or at least alphabetical sections of a large directory, they were permitted to arrive at work earlier or to leave later, so long as they worked their standard week. Almost all elected to come to work earlier, a few later. This practice resulted in better office coverage and better utilization of office machines than was previously the case. The job, the work itself, was not changed, but control of it by the clerks was improved.

STRATEGY: *When employees at a particular job show signs of excessive tardiness, absence, or goofing-off, examine the design of the job. Consider changing hours as part of a larger job strategy, not as an item of bribery.*

PRINCIPLE 18: If unions accurately represent the wishes of their members, they are likely to favor job design efforts that result in jobs of greater quality.

DISCUSSION: Experience with the two major unions in the communications industry (CWA and IBEW) supports this. When one of the improved jobs (directory-clerical) resulted in the opening of a higher job classification for those who had accepted responsibility for whole directories, this lent positive reinforcement to the union leaders as well as to the clerks. As early as 1973, contacts and correspondence with Douglas A. Fraser, now president of the United Auto Workers, revealed that this union was eager to help managements in their efforts to improve the quality of jobs in the automobile industry. The national contract that year, in fact, provided for the joint financing of certain costs. At the same time, the United Mine Workers made concessions to the owners of the Rushton coal mine near Johnstown, Pennsylvania, that facilitated the owners' effort to improve working arrangements in the mine. In effect, the union permitted the formation of semi-autonomous mini-groups among miners.* I'm sure there must be many other unions that have supported similar efforts. The unions in Scandinavian countries have gone far beyond American unions in actively supporting efforts to make work interesting, with the Swedish experience especially well documented.†

STRATEGY: *Collaborate with the unions in redesigning jobs or in laying out new work configurations. This is usually the very best time for making a "new deal" in the workplace, especially if union-management relations are not too tense. If relations are bad, go ahead anyhow to show good intent on management's part, and bet that the union will support the effort in the long run. When and if the economy faces a downturn, expect the union to revert to the defense of its members on traditional "bread-and-butter" issues, such as layoffs and seniority. But give your union a chance to contribute in a statesmanlike way to this effort at good job design.*

Job Cycles

PRINCIPLE 19: Though advances in technology could be used to provide jobs of better quality, they usually bring about the automation of some parts of a job, resulting in fragmentation of the module and job dissatisfaction.

DISCUSSION: In the numerous job enrichment trials aimed at improving the clerical job in compiling telephone directories, we discovered that a new computerized proce-

*I. Bluestone, "Decision Making by Workers," *Personnel Administration,* July–August 1974. S. Klaidman, "Coal Miners Doing Their Own Thing," *Washington Post,* January 25, 1976. "When Miners Try to Boss Themselves," *Business Week,* February 2, 1976.

†The Swedish Employers' Confederation, Box 16120, S–103–23, Stockholm, Sweden, has published a number of reports, such as: "Job Reform in Sweden—Conclusions from 500 Shop Floor Projects," 1975 (an excellent summary); "The Volvo Report," 1975; "The Saab-Scania Report," 1973; "Autonomous Groups and Payment by Results," 1973.

dure—whereby the customer information for directories would be stored in and printed by a computer—could lead to a significant reduction in job quality from the employees' point of view. If employees had to give up their individual directories and become adjuncts of the computer, it would be a loss for them. Many enjoyed getting out their own directories. The solution was to keep the one book–one clerk approach and to train the clerks to use the computer. The position we should take on the issue of technological advances is this: We must arrange it so that the advance becomes a tool of the employee and not the other way around.

STRATEGY: *Hold off the introduction of automation for part of a job until a whole, new job, complete with automation, feedback, and control, can be designed for the worker. Favor new work arrangements that call for employees to learn new skills, such as operating the new cathode ray tubes in the Ferguson Telephone District example cited earlier. Establish a guidance committee for the introduction of new equipment or systems, composed of (1) laboratory and design people, (2) people from the department that will receive the new setup, (3) a job design specialist.*

PRINCIPLE 20: When a job consists of fragments, the leftovers from a previously whole job, that job will be less motivating than it was when it was whole.

DISCUSSION: Examples of fragmented jobs may be those of making change in a vending machine area or near telephone booths at an airport, operating an almost completely automated elevator, operating a yarn-balling machine, so nearly automated that the operators continually fall asleep.

STRATEGY: *Either automate a job completely or include the remaining fragments in a larger service job. For example, as new equipment enables customers to perform more and more of the work of placing telephone calls, we need to find a way to combine the remaining tasks (intercepting and helping when people make mistakes, dial numbers that have been disconnected, want to make credit card calls, collect calls, information requests, trouble reports, etc.) into a full-service traffic operator's position. In fact, this effort is in progress now in the Bell System, with a "good job" as one of the explicit objectives, along with economy, accuracy, and speedy service. If this cannot be done, one can only hope to find usable tradeoffs, such as money, benefits, gliding time, the four-day week, coffee breaks, and sympathy. What is the risk to the job to which the leftover task is added? There is some, and problems should be watched for, but there seems to be less danger in adding fragments to most tasks than in subtracting large pieces from them, especially if the additions have a natural relation to the whole.*

PRINCIPLE 21: Employees will tend to become less motivated as their jobs become fragmented.

DISCUSSION: This observation is supported by Chapter 2, "Why Jobs Die," which is the focus of this book. Most of us are confronted daily with experiences that illustrate this principle at work. For example, in the small town where I lived for many years, our garageman and his three assistants took in the troubled car, diagnosed it, fixed it, and, if you asked, gave it a routine tune-up, oil change, and greasing. Service was complete and excellent. In my current location, one person writes up the work order, another takes the car to a storage area, and the car works its way eventually to an engine specialist, a transmission man, lube man, tire man, and a car wash rack. There is a separate parts desk. The service manager computes the bill, passes it through a window to a bookkeeper, who verifies it and calls your name on a loudspeaker. If you can pay, someone goes to the storage lot for the car. As is to be expected, service is not good. After four years, I know none of the people who service my car, and they don't know me. A sign warns me to keep out of the service area. They have had two strikes, with many grievances other than money, and three service managers. In my view, the cause of this unhappy situation—unhappy not only for customers but also for the employees—is excessive fragmentation of the work.

STRATEGY: *Don't let fragmentation occur if it can possibly be avoided. In fact, build jobs up as time passes and new technology becomes available. Encourage employees to acquire new skills. If fragmentation cannot be prevented, try to include the remaining job in a larger job or in a mini-group. Or move the long-term employee to new work and hire beginners with qualifications more in line with the demands of the job as it now exists.*

PRINCIPLE 22: A job involving equipment that challenges an employee over a relatively long period of time will be more attractive to employees than a job with equipment that can be mastered readily.

DISCUSSION: A piano with one or two octaves is not as challenging as one with 88 notes. To many musicians an organ with its many manuals and foot pedals is even more challenging. Similarly, a good job should have many levels of challenge built into it.

STRATEGY: *We must learn how to design and build equipment and jobs that use the equipment in such a way that boredom and monotony are held off for a long time, if not indefinitely. The ideal piece of equipment would be built around a complete module of activity, a meaningful act as the employee sees it. Control would be with the employee. And the device would be adequately loaded with feedback mechanisms so that the employee could monitor his or her own performance.*

5

redesigning jobs for motivation

IN THE LAST 10 OR 15 YEARS, I have accumulated enough wounds from projects that failed to enable me to offer some suggestions that may help managers avoid failure. This chapter will concentrate on sources of help in getting a design or redesign effort started, but the ideas should also help managers to avoid setting up bad jobs in a new work flow. The next chapter offers a prescription for maintaining the motivational thrust, once it's started. These chapters are not intended to replace the two basic chapters "The Art of Reshaping Jobs" (Chapter 7) and "Following Through to an Improved Job" (Chapter 8) in my earlier book.* These chapters dealt with actual techniques of running meetings and conducting follow-up procedures. When the situation fits, those techniques are still recommended, but we have more experience now and some new ideas about how to begin a job design effort.

Look for Trouble Signs

"How do I know whether *my* jobs are dying? In fact, how do I know that one wasn't stillborn?" The following

*Motivation Through the Work Itself, New York: AMACOM, 1969.

should help you perform a weak-spot analysis. There are many telltale signs of possible trouble. Here are some major ones. In a real sense, an organization is like a finely built engine. Engines seldom fail "suddenly." They emit signals well in advance that something is going wrong; then they quit. Are you getting signals? What follows are families of symptoms. If a family of symptoms causes you and your associates to repeatedly think of one or a few locations or work groups, you may have found an excellent place to start a work redesign effort.

BUSYNESS

People not busy:

There is work to be done, but "It's someone else's work."

Need to make work, wondering to yourself, "What can I give this person to do?"

People doing crossword puzzles, chatting.

People too busy:

Endless information meetings to get "the word," to coordinate, to reach decisions.

Going from meeting to meeting.

Meeting off-hours, at night—"The only time we can do it."

No time to plan; always on an emergency footing.

Managers doing clerical or craft work in order to make deadlines.

Deadlines being met with blood, sweat, and tears.

RESPONSIBILITY

No one has it (or it's two or three levels above the operator level):

Work moving from location to location or pool to pool, in assembly-line fashion, instead of within the mini-group.

Responsibility for a given machine divided among maintenance, set-up, materials flow people, overhaul, production control, quality control. To make a decision three to six people must meet.

Long, branching work-flow designs.

No one wants it:
"Don't tell me; tell them." (Buck passing)
No one "reaching" to help a customer/client.
People feel impotent:
"My problem is that *I have no immediate problem.* I know
I worked all day, but I just can't tell you what I did."
"Nothing here really bugs me. Oh, yes, there are prob-
lems, but they are not mine."

PERFORMANCE
Productivity:
"Great, but we are behind ..."
"Trouble-shooters" exist other than employees, so as to
not stop production.
"Expediters," another new job because work is not going
out.
Excessive overtime, costly production.
Quality:
Productivity up, but the quality so poor that shipments
are off.
Quality control being done by other than the originating
person or the mini-group.
Work being done twice, reprocessing.
Service:
Increasing number of customer complaints.
Customers exasperated with company or organization
when they finally run the maze.
Customers writing or contacting very high levels in order
to get service, or writing to Congresspeople.
Company finding it necessary to advertise that its service
is great: "If only the public understood ..."

UNIONS
Growth of unions where economic issues are not the
reason.
Grievances, especially trivial ones.
Anger, ill feelings, hostility long after economic issues are
settled, long after it is clear to everyone that the final

offer is on the table (perhaps the contract is one that has been ratified by similar workers elsewhere, which indicates that it is reasonable).

Management persistently offering money, benefits, time off, vacations, and other maintenance items in an effort to buy quality.

PERSONNEL SYMPTOMS

Management Jobs:

Growing in size, relative to nonmanagement.

New layers, added height to the pyramid.

Half-level titles and jobs beginning to appear, e.g., "assistant to the division manager."

"Façade" titles—special assignments manager, director of _____, executive officer—when there is already a full complement of regular chairpeople, presidents, vice presidents, etc. These "façade" titles should have a statute of limitations.

Lots of new titles; as many titles as there are people.

One-on-one management reporting.

Titles that indicate the job is primarily a control job, not a creative one.

"Dotted line" reporting relationships; multiple bosses.

Nonmanagement Jobs:

Jobs failing to disappear after new equipment or systems are introduced, as was promised, and lots of explanations such as "ironing out bugs"; "shakedown trips" or preliminary try-outs that last forever.

Management itself conceding in private, "That's a poor job. I worked on it myself during the last strike."

Lack of interest in jobs, as evidenced by high rates of turnover, absenteeism, tardiness, complaints and grievances, requests for time off.

FINANCIAL SYMPTOMS

Product lines or services no longer profitable; you have priced yourself out of the market.

Personnel costs escalating.

Work being farmed out to other firms or locations because "They can do it cheaper." Why?

Using outsiders when the work to be done is not the result of increased or unusual demand (peaks and valleys), but because you are beginning to lose control of your workforce.

Searching for a "grateful population," threatening to move plants to get away from "the kind of people we have around here."

New small competitors succeeding when their advantage could not be due to better technology or experience; they may have a more meaningful work flow.

NON-JOB SOLUTIONS

Each of the following managerial techniques is designed to make job problems go away. If you find you have bought in on them, look for a more fundamental cause and some changes that just might work—look at the jobs themselves.

Communications:

"You have a communications problem." When related jobs are designed so poorly that human communication has become impossible, communication is neither the cause nor the solution. Redesign the work, make communication a natural thing again.

Two-way communications meetings. The assumption is that the work is fundamentally okay, but somebody doesn't understand something.

Skip-level meetings. Your boss talks to your reporting people, with you absent.

"Talk back" sessions. The boss promises to try to answer any question.

Strong need to get the message down to the troops. Why is the situation not evident, why does management have to explain it?

Attitude Surveys:

Administered principally to help "them" get "it" off their chests, as opposed to surveys that are part of a before-and-after measurement plan.

Administered in the hope that employees know what's wrong, because you don't.

Human Relations Training:

Human relations persistently alleged to be the trouble.

Basic training: Be nice to people.

Advanced training: Understand, be empathetic, be sensitive, so that your employees will adjust to their work.

Clue: Why is it generally unnecessary for townspeople or the members of a family to take human relations training, but we must do it relentlessly at our workplaces?

Make a Formal Analysis

A former colleague, David A. Whitsett, urges the manager to make a formal analysis of the organization chart and work-flow diagrams in a search for deficient situations. If no structural weaknesses are evident, there is little hope that job redesign will help. In his helpful article, Whitsett* points not only to some of the trouble signs mentioned above—such as the creation of the jobs of checker, expediter, coordinator, control clerk, troubleshooter, communications clerk, and specialist—but, in addition, challenges odd reporting relationships that may be revealed by standard organizational charts, such as:

—One boss who is reported to by only one supervisor, who in turn is responsible for many people. What does that upper boss do—boss one person?

—One boss who reports to two bosses in parallel boxes. Below the one boss come many people. Who is really the boss of this operation? What does the boss in the other box do?

—The "specialist" in a block all alone. The person doesn't have any reporting people, but is high up in the organization. There is a good chance that this "super-guru's" job robs other jobs of responsibility.

---

*"Where Are Your Unenriched Jobs?" *Harvard Business Review,* January–February 1975, pp. 74–80.

—No clear reporting relationship or duty, as evidenced by dotted lines or vague placement on the chart.

—Reporting relationships and job titles indicating very small differences in the jobs: junior claims analyst, claims analyst, claims reviewer, etc. (Whitsett gives 11 titles in one series.)

Whitsett and I share the following thought: "Show me a pool and I'll show you trouble" (e.g., typing pool, drafting center, motor pool, reproduction pool). In addition, we both find complicated work flows an indicator that trouble may be brewing.

If you have indeed located a trouble spot after making both informal and formal searches for trouble signs, ideas for improving the situation will start surfacing. A good manager can't live with a bad job situation. But how to rectify it? We know the model and the principles for good jobs. How do we get there?

Who Is to Conduct the Redesign Effort?

There is only one good answer to this question: the person who is managing that job, the level directly above the job. If the manager is not sold on the prospect, little improvement can be hoped for. How, then, are we to sell the manager these concepts in job design, of functional completeness, of consistency, with power to act and adequate feedback? Having the manager memorize the concepts will be of no help, and upper levels can't order line managers to follow them.

If direct managers of work flows and their jobs are to be reached as a partial step in improving those work flows and jobs, the managers will need a chance to absorb the concepts intellectually and emotionally, that is, they will need to both understand them and believe in them. The usual avenues of education come into play:

> Lectures (not too effective).
> Seminars and workshops (better by far).

Reading material.
Paper-and-pencil cases and exercises.
Test material.

The last three are vital to the success of any seminar.

It is always a challenge to plan such a management development effort and tailor it to the needs and the background of a particular organization. This could be the first task for a "key person," someone to help the manager who may not have the necessary extra time to do it. Especially in medium-size or larger organizations, a key person is the one to get the effort moving, supported, of course, by the boss's clear signals of wanting the management team to become skillful in the design and organization of work. In a small organization, or even in larger ones, where there is not much support as yet for such an effort, managers may have to be their own key people. The remainder of this chapter is addressed to the key people, the ones who are going to start the redesign effort, be they specially assigned to the project or the managers themselves.

Key People and Their Job

In my experience successful key people have come from all parts of an organization. In larger organizations where there may be several key people, a diversity of background is all to the good when they have reason to assist each other in a training effort, in the careful analysis of a work flow, or in the actual perpetration of a change. I've seen them come from the branches of engineering, the behavioral sciences, business administration, from anywhere in management.

The characteristics they are likely to have are: (1) Sufficient intelligence and academic success to enable them to handle the college-level concepts in this field comfortably. (2) The ability to present job redesign ideas well and to persuade managers to try them. (3) Dedication to the field of job redesign. This should grow naturally; it is not a prerequisite to the work. (4) A record of tenacity in accomplishing work, for perseverance will be needed in this endeavor.

Key people need not have great knowledge of the jobs in the organization. They may come from outside the organization, in fact, if no one is available inside. Openness to new modes of thinking rather than great knowledge of how work has been done is the order of the day.

No doubt the job of the key person has been largely revealed by the list of characteristics. Key people must be acceptable to an organization so that they can get to the top of the pyramid and then down into its roots if the job design and work organization effort is to pay off. (If the managers are the key people, and they can encapsulate their own efforts at redesign themselves, then this job requirement is of no importance, unless job changes or results begin to affect organizations other than the manager's own.) Naturally, in order to deal with the top of the organization and its roots, the key person must be skilled at assembling ideas and making presentations. I know of no shortcuts to this, so I will discuss some problems that are frequently encountered in these endeavors and make suggestions for surmounting them.

The key person's job may be viewed as merely transitional, lasting two to four years while the line managers gain the necessary knowledge and skill in job design and work organization. In medium- to large-size organizations where new products and equipment are always coming on stream, the key person may easily become the catalyst of a small task force whose job is to assure a good work flow and good job slices. This can be a full-time, permanent assignment involving updating the current job design and work organization and assuring the future. Whether a transitional appointment, a full-time job, or a project for the on-line managers themselves acting as their own key people, certain common problems must be confronted. One of the first will be getting backing within the organization. Here are some proven ideas.

HOW TO GET HELP FROM TOP MANAGEMENT

Although much has been said in the last ten years about job enrichment, many top bosses will know little or nothing about it. They may not know that total job redesign and work organization rather than job enrichment is the thrust now recommended. Therefore, a day's session should be proposed in which the idea and the evidence for redesigning old jobs is presented clearly. Chapters 1 and 2 of this book may provide a framework for the key person. Some examples of successful redesign should be presented, involving work flows not too different from those in your organization. It is unlikely that you will find examples with identical work flows.

In addition to presenting the problem of poor job design, conditions that cause jobs to get sick and die, give the bosses a chance to redesign an existing job, using case examples now available. This is, of course, an *analytic* approach. The boss is introduced to the concepts of the complete job, the motivating assignment (to be found in Chapter 3), and invited to redesign a job situation, such as keypunch, the operation of a bagging machine, directory compilation, or the job of workers on a typewriter assembly line. In the cases I have presented in similar situations, the criterion is not what we think should be an ideal design, but the successful design actually worked out by a group of supervisors. Three examples of such cases are presented in the Appendix to this book.

This approach to informing the bosses is a reasonably close approximation to the "clinical pathological conference" used for years by outstanding medical schools, wherein the objective is to help the student learn what causes patients to live or die. In our clinical cases, the "patient" always lives. These cases are very appealing to bosses and need to become more widely used. Bosses will likely favor training of managers at lower levels if they (the bosses) are also given a chance to diagnose some actual cases of "sick jobs."

Involving the top bosses in working on some actual cases will help you in enlisting their support. They will see the practicality and depth of the proposed training, which must go beyond work motivation theory, platitudes, and such abstract concepts as giving employees responsibility and opportunities for achievement, recognition, and psychological growth. The aim of good job design is to ensure that a job situation has these characteristics, but the language is too abstract for working purposes. A functionally complete and consistent module, with reasonable control and plenty of feedback—these are more concrete concepts.

Another approach to redesigning a job or work flow that has repeatedly been successful in enlisting the support of all levels of management is the *green-light* or *brainstorming session.* As part of a seminar on job redesign, and after only two or three hours, top management can be challenged to name a few jobs within their control that seem to need attention. As an example, offer them the job of "your secretary" but say you will use it as the objective of green-lighting only as a last resort. They will probably come up with three to six jobs of their own. List them on an easel pad. Ask for a show of hands as to which job concerns them most—which might indeed be a candidate for redesign or improvement.

Now to the green-light session. Ask the bosses to toss out ideas for improving that one job as fast as you can write them. There is one simple rule: No one is allowed to throw a red light on someone else's green-light item. Participants may not emit any signs of disapproval of someone else's item—no gasping in agony, falling off the chair, turning around to stare, no disapproval at all. They will almost always laugh and accept the assignment in good spirit. You may have to be firm, pointing out a violation of the green-light rule should one occur, but usually the conferees will remind each other, "You just threw a red light on me." Easel sheets are torn off and hung on the wall, for further stimulation and reference. Conferees are encouraged to add a "tail to someone else's dog," to extend or refine someone else's item. Unless it's done merely to contradict or to "red-light" someone else, the reverse of an item might be offered.

Sometimes these meetings are called "creative thinking" sessions. Green-lighting is less pretentious, especially since the thrust of many items and the final product may be to return a job to the shape it had several years earlier, when it was indeed a good job.

How long should this green-lighting continue? If the seminar involves only green-lighting, a demonstration of half an hour can be very useful. But if this is a *workshop,* called to consider the restructuring of a work flow and its jobs, the green-light session may go on for hours, or it may end while the conferees start "red-lighting," or evaluating the items.

The right to red-light an item, to disagree with a proposal, must frequently be promised conferees in order to keep the green-lighting alive. When green-lighting dies down naturally, the time is ripe for evaluating the items. After a trial run at evaluating a few items, the conferees will usually opt for approaching the task using one or two subgroups, and attention will shift toward getting the right people into the right subgroup. At this stage the workshop may adjourn. Ideally, a firm date is set for reviewing the progress and the recommendations of the subgroups.

If a new job or group of jobs is about to come into existence in the organization, consider using it as the basis for an analytical examination, a green-light examination, or a combination of the two. Will this new job be a good job for employees, or will it be boring and meaningless to them? Such a question followed by a short work period, with the promise that lower levels of management will go through the same process in greater length and depth, should help win top management's approval for starting a job redesign effort somewhere within the organization.

This strategy for getting the attention and support of the top bosses relies on their actually sampling the training. It does not ask them to support job design or redesign simply as an article of faith and goodwill. At its best, green-lighting may help the key person demonstrate to upper management that there are, indeed, jobs that need attention (they have listed a few and worked on one) and that a tested, new point of view on work motivation now exists to help them redesign current jobs or to block the creation of poor jobs. You ask for their blessing and support in furthering the effort. Even if it is immediately given, you'd better prepare yourself for dark days, when some new pronouncement emanates from this same topside, ordering or forbidding something that is really an employee's responsibility. At this point you may say to yourself, "I wonder if they heard a word I said?"

This strategy is no panacea, of course. Topside must become acquainted with the nature of this effort, and contradictory policies may emerge at first. But if this does occur, it will be a lot easier to get them reconciled now that all levels have participated in seminars or workshops.

WORK WITH "FAMILIES" OF SUPERVISORS

Once top management accepts the idea that the job design and work organization effort might help, the key person should switch from working with cross-sectional groups (managers from various departments or organizations who are attending seminars) to working exclusively with supervisory "families." A family is composed of all the supervisors reporting to one manager. Two, three, or more levels of supervision may be involved. At this stage the meetings change character significantly. The objective is no longer to inform or win friends or customers for a job design or redesign effort but to get such an effort actually started. To put it differently, the meetings now are in the nature of *workshops* rather than seminars.

There is great merit in insisting on the presence of the entire family, the whole pyramid of supervisors responsible for the job under discussion, or at least as many as can possibly attend the two- or three-day workshops. They are the ones who ultimately must make the changes, if any, and who know the details of the job and the work flow. In fact, many of them may even have held that job at an earlier time in their careers. By including the whole family, the supervisors will have a hand in the decision as to what will actually be attempted and when and how changes are to be introduced. And because they were all in attendance at the same meeting, they will not return to a possibly hostile group of other supervisors who are skeptical of the entire job design or redesign effort.

A recurring reason for the failure of job design seminars with attendants from many different organizations is that no one back home really understands or cares about what went on in the seminar. Obviously, the seminars, whose objective is to inform and persuade, are just as important as the "family workshops," for if the seminar is unsuccessful, there will be no workshop and, in my experience, little or no results. The job of the key person is to switch from the seminar format to a workshop approach as soon as some managers say, "Let's go." Key people generally report that conducting seminars can be fun; but the workshop is where the real payoff will occur.

OFFER TO HELP MANAGERS REDESIGN THEIR OWN JOBS

The biggest spur to the spread of these job design concepts, in my personal experience at the headquarters of a large corporation, was entirely unplanned—by me, at least. There's a lesson in it for smaller organizations, too. First, what happened? Then let us see if we can generalize.

After a number of fairly successful job redesign efforts were at hand for such basic jobs as keypunch, service representatives, and installer–repairpeople, the representatives of a headquarters middle management group quietly asked if a redesign session could be held on a certain key job that existed in their own location at headquarters. Did not these principles apply to management jobs, also?

The answer was yes. The only troublesome question

was: How will we know objectively if we have succeeded in improving this particular middle management job? Someone proposed that an attitude questionnaire might be used before the session started, and then again nine months to a year later. This might provide some evidence, but would anyone believe it? What hard evidence—dollar results or productivity, for example—could be dreamed up for the measurement of headquarters' staff jobs? Changes would occur, we expected, but so slowly that two or three years might elapse before we would know objectively whether our sessions had caused the difference.

The decision was reached: "We are going to go ahead. We are adults, trying to improve the design of our very own jobs, and we'll make the judgment of success or failure as we do all the time—a common-sense judgment." These men and women and their bosses spent two days in a workshop (designed as in the preceding sections) and then went through the follow-up procedures outlined in the next chapter. Key people were assigned to help any group that wanted to run such sessions at headquarters and to help with following through to completion, actually getting changes made in these crucial middle management jobs.

As was said earlier, here, if anywhere, is where the *bosses* of the job being redesigned are likely to smile and say, "I learned from this that it was *my* job that was being redesigned." Often, indeed, there would be no possible way of redesigning the job under analysis without removing responsibilities and duties that had worked their way upward to the boss of the job.

Long before any hard results were at hand, other headquarters groups asked for similar workshops until more than 50 organizational units were involved. (The seminar stage was actually skipped at headquarters, thanks to books, articles, in-house publications, and the grapevine.) This called for more than 40 two-day sessions—quite an investment of time, money, and effort. How much good was done for these essentially unmeasurable jobs will never be known objectively. The fact that group after group voluntarily asked for similar sessions may be the best evidence of positive results we will ever have.

One thing is certain: These managers, in their dealings with colleagues in the field, became the best possible carriers of the message that headquarters believes in job redesign and is working at it, and expects these considerations in designing good jobs to become a way of life, not to be just a temporary program. Generalizing from this experience, my advice to key people is: Get to headquarters groups as soon as you can.

Elsewhere I have said that the key person should avoid "unmeasurable" jobs if possible, since the lack of proof of effectiveness might lead to disbelief or even ridicule. Now I say, come to an agreement on this unfortunate fact if the jobs to be improved are management jobs at headquarters. Then knock yourself out trying to help them *improve their own jobs.* The spinoff, the help they can give in spreading and utilizing the concepts as they then go about their field work is very great indeed. Expect some cynicism such as, "I don't know how much good you people did for my job, but let me tell you about a task force I'm working on. I know that the jobs we are creating are now going to be better jobs." Such cynicism, we can afford. At this point I am reminded of an aphorism from Plutarch: "The human mind is not a vessel to be filled, but a fire to be lighted."

HELP MANAGERS WORK ON ANY JOB

Once top management has accepted these motivational concepts as a way of life—even if they occasionally fall from grace—and once middle managers have struggled to redesign their own jobs or any job in their departments, the key person should shift to a new role. As key person, you should demote yourself half a step. If managers come to you for assistance with problem jobs, offer to help them run workshops to deal with them. They have each sat through a workshop. Now let them make the presentation *as far as possible*—run the projector if slides or films are to be used, put suggestions on the easel pad if green-lighting is employed, or start the diagramming of the work flow if the basic approach is analytic rather than green-lighting. (It can be either, or a combination of the two.)

Let the managers make assignments if further work must be done, which is almost always the case. Let them set goals and target dates. Offer to help, and to get help, especially if interdepartmental problems arise. You are now a resource person. If you can accomplish this transfer, this approach to job design and work organization is on its way into the corporation's bloodstream.

DEPEND ON MANAGERS TO WORK ON NEW JOBS

The ideas for new equipment, new systems, new procedures, and new methods are likely to originate at headquarters or to be channeled through headquarters from the laboratories or from outside suppliers, on the way to the field. If you as the key person can enlist the minds—and the hearts—of the headquarters people, you are well on your way toward making a significant, lasting contribution to the organization. The best time to introduce good job design concepts into an organization is at the moment when new work flows are first being discussed. Don't hang back if invited; get in early. In fact, try to get yourself invited; offer to help.

Don't be surprised if the effort becomes formalized. For example, at this time in the organization I know best, teams actually exist for the sole purpose of looking at new jobs, new equipment, new systems, with the aim of maximizing the job quality for future employees. The teams usually consist of a laboratory or a design person, a representative of the department that will eventually receive the job, the equipment, or the system, and a representative of the human resources development group. The teams disappear when the new job and/or system is in operation, of course. Then it's up to the operating department to run it as well as possible.

COMPLETE THE FEASIBILITY STUDY

Assume now that you, as either manager or key person, want to go ahead on a job redesign effort in your own department or that you have been asked to help someone else in his or her department. If you have thought about the situation in light of the discussion in this chapter thus far, much of a formal feasibility study has been completed. The following eight items are to remind you of a variety of questions that need to be answered before starting out:

1. What is the present state of employees' satisfaction or dissatisfaction with their work? My preference is to conduct some in-depth interviews with the first-level bosses and a sample of the employees rather than to use a formal questionnaire.

2. Are wages and/or the incentive system so bad that they would hopelessly impede attempts to change a work situation? If so, fix them first.

3. What is the environment, other than the work itself —the quality and potential of the supervisors, their interest in the proposed project, company policies that might hinder or help, possibility of changing something (or is this a huge, expensive, heavily capitalized situation, with jobs and consoles hopelessly fixed)?

4. How good or bad are the interpersonal relations among management people? Is there hope for improvement? (There is no reason to ask that they be good, merely that they not be impossibly bad.)

5. What is the union–management situation? Is something imminent, such as bargaining, that will affect the chances for success? Is there an internal union squabble? Might the union help, or at least not hinder, if approached skillfully? In my own experience, both major unions with which the Bell System bargained (CWA and IBEW) asked to be in on site selection and on strategy matters once they learned that job redesign was aimed at working smarter, not harder, and that rewards—if any—would become an issue for discussion in the next bargaining session.

6. Is there likelihood that a job design or redesign effort might tie in nicely with contemplated changes? Have job layouts and assignments been finalized, or are they still in flux? Does a work group have to be moved because of a space problem? Consider moving the group that could be part of a job redesign effort.

7. Is the job measurable? How will we know whether employees are performing better or worse than before? If performance goals and work standards don't exist now, can they be set up as part of the job redesign effort? If this is not possible, can there be agreement on what will be acceptable results (see the next section also)?

8. Is the productivity problem actually outside the control of the group whose work is being redesigned? Should other work groups be part of the effort from the start? Can they be expected to cooperate?

GET HELP FROM A GOAL-SETTING SESSION

Numerous remarks have been made about the importance of deciding in advance whether there is a chance for success and what the criteria will be. This is a feasibility item (No. 7 in the preceding list). Nothing will make the key person's life easier than clear-cut evidence that this approach to work organization pays off. This section summarizes the four major goals, four ways in which a payoff can occur. They should be discussed openly by the workshop participants.

1. *Improved productivity.* This is a major goal, whether a service is being performed or a product is being turned out. How will we know if productivity improves?

2. *Improved human satisfaction with work.* How will we know? Our reason for having this as a possible goal is clear: We want to improve human work motivation. Why? Because we are motivated toward, we tend to move toward, those things we like, unless something diverts us. In addition to having employees motivated by money, benefits, buildings, policies, and so forth, we want them to be increasingly motivated by this job under redesign, to

find more psychological reward from what they now do and the way they do it than was previously the case. We can determine this by a combination of such items as: quit rates, absences, tardiness, whether current employees bring desirable potential employees to the company, job satisfaction questionnaires, and employee interviews. The last two have to be performed both before and after the project is under way if their results are to be meaningful. The supervisory team will probably be the best source of ideas on possible measures of human satisfaction.

In one location where a study was about to start, the bosses specified "reduction of union grievances" as the measure of increased job satisfaction, because they were averaging 50 to 55 grievances per year. In some other locations, formal grievances were so seldom registered that other measures had to be employed.

Although human satisfaction at work was not specified as the prime purpose in these situations, it is clear that there will probably be no improvements in productivity, service, quality, and promptness of work unless employees feel better, in the long run, about their tasks. Therefore, this is an objective of the job design or redesign effort.

3. *Improved customer reaction.* Remember, customers may be internal to a business as well as external. The engineering and the drafting departments have customers just as do the sales and marketing departments. And if possible, customer reaction should be measured. Depending on the job, there will surely be measures such as sales; returned goods; complaints, commendations (letters, telephone calls); bad, or good, free publicity; customer surveys, interviews, questionnaires. Internal customers or clients can be just as happy or unhappy as external clients. A little imagination will likely produce a way of telling whether interdepartmental cooperation and attitudes have improved or deteriorated.

4. *Greater ease of management.* I doubt that responsible

managers would start a job redesign project merely to make their own jobs easier. However, bosses almost invariably talk about the improved control that they get when the job redesign effort has been successful.

Perhaps greater ease of management will not be a stated objective, but it need not be an item on the hidden agenda. The likelihood is high in a successful study, judged by hard results, that the boss and the managers will find that they need not police the employees as much to get production, that mini-groups or, as in the IBM plant, mini-lines will tend to run themselves when the boss is called away.

At one time I made some calculations in Illinois Bell as to what jobs were likely to be dropped in a successful job redesign project. The trial group was the directory compilation group, which decreased from 120 to 74 persons. That remarkable 38 percent drop included both management and nonmanagement people. Two conclusions were striking: (1) Proportionately more management people were reassigned to other work than nonmanagement people. (2) Of the management people reassigned, more staff persons were reassigned than line managers. Line managers are still needed; however, the first-line manager might start reporting directly to a third-line boss. Or "half-levels" of line managers might be dropped. Clearly, however, there was less need for such staff persons as "methods," "results," "analysis," "procedures," and similar specialists; at least they were no longer needed on a full-time basis.

Since that field trial, many others have been completed in various places. Many times I have heard confirmation of the original findings that more people are reassigned from the management than from the nonmanagement workforce. Seldom does it ever reach 38 percent, however. If the work flow can be changed from person-to-person or station-to-station, perhaps under different bosses, to one where an individual or a mini-group completes the whole job, then the key person should be prepared to find force reductions of this order: 15–20 percent among nonmanagement, clerical, craft workers; 20–25 percent among management workers. The key person will be taxed to demonstrate the effectiveness of the projects. Be prepared. Ordinary measures of cost improvements may not be complete. For example, supervision is often not included as a direct cost in work measurement, and a reduction in this important cost won't be reported, unless the key person makes certain that it is.

After going through the four goals of a job redesign effort, some skeptic may say, "Yes, but what is the *real* reason behind this proposed effort? It's just to make more money for the company, isn't it?" The direct answer is this: There is no *one* real reason. Nobody should object to a handsome payoff for a job redesign effort, such as an obvious reduction in waste or expense. No one should object if customers, employees, and managers all feel better about the project after it has progressed for a while. Success in any one or any combination of the four goals is fine. But if the effort is costly, we can safely predict that the organization will kill the project unless it can afford the expense.

ENLIST THE HELP OF SPECIALISTS

Certain specialized persons or groups can help the key person or the manager immensely in going ahead with the job design effort. The laboratory person, designing consoles to be operated by employees, is one such person. Another is the "human factors" person who ensures that a human being can operate the equipment, and helps answer a different question: not *can* employees operate this thing, but *will* they do it, willingly, or will the job call for blood, sweat, and tears? The methods and procedures people and the software specialists are others who can help.

As indicated earlier, the best and fastest way to get their support may be through offering to work with them on their jobs. If a workshop on their jobs seems out of place, suggest at least a half-day seminar, such as the one presented to top management. People who work on new equipment or methods are so intelligent, in my experience, that little urging is required to get their help in extending this point of view to the design of jobs or systems on which they may be working. A seminar can be the start of a long relationship with these important people.

CONSIDER USING OUTSIDE HELP

Generally, a corporation will need some outside assistance until its own key people are trained. The key people can then become the "outsiders" for suborganizations of the corporation until they put themselves out of business.

There are still not very many consulting firms or persons who have actual experience in job redesign. One should be very strict in reviewing the qualifications of a proposed "outsider" for this work. Qualifications such as these are open to suspicion:

> Employee attitude specialist.
> Employee communications specialist.
> Personnel systems consultant.
> Psychological, or sociological, consultant.

That last one described me, in fact. Until I had struggled through some failures and successes, help from me would have been minimal although my motives were excellent.

What I'm saying is: Be wary of people who offer only general titles as credentials. To be helpful, these people must know, *specifically*, the literature of job design— some of the books mentioned in the Bibliography, for example. Ask what books they have read in this field. And they must be interested in continuing to investigate the subject. Many of the authors listed in the Bibliography, for example, are journalists, with no interest in undertaking projects on their own; in fact, they may have long since moved on to new areas of journalism, as is quite proper.

THE INDUSTRIAL ENGINEER—A SPECIAL CASE

The most hopeful sign that I see on the horizon is that industrial engineers are taking an interest in job design. As Serge A. Birn said in the Foreword, a marriage is long overdue between behavioral scientists and the industrial engineer who has traditionally been responsible for this field. The key person may find help here. The problem of motivation and the road to follow in making jobs desirable psychologically are now well marked. This need not extend by one day the training of the engineer still in college, and the deficiencies in training among practicing engineers can be repaired in seminars and workshops. The concept of follow-up education for professionally trained and certified people is spreading rapidly; job design and work organization from the human point of view would make a natural subject.

TRY TO CHANGE THE SITUATION, NOT PEOPLE'S ATTITUDES

Scott Myers, who reported striking success with job redesign when he was organizational psychologist for Texas Instruments, once remarked: "When people feel they belong to an organization, they tend to support its systems." Perhaps this should be added to the list of principles in Chapter 4. Now the question becomes, How do we get employees to feel that they belong to the organization? If we are going to redesign some jobs—perhaps form a mini-group if that seems called for—how do we act so that the employees will work toward and with the proposed changes?

Let me mention again various ways that have been tried in an effort to change employee attitudes, and then offer a newer philosophy for winning support: We have tried human relations training for supervisors (be decent with your people), one-way communication (films, company magazines, newsletters, papers, bulletin boards, closed-circuit TV), two-way communication (questionnaires, suggestion plans, face-to-face meetings of many kinds), a thousand varieties of benefit plans as well as straight wages, contests and prizes ("zero defects," "pride in performance," etc.), out-of-hours programs, beautification of the work environment, democracy in the workplace, employee representation on boards of directors. The list goes on and on.

In no way do I consider these techniques unworthy; I merely wish to point out that the strategy underlying these approaches to winning employee support for the organization's goals suffers from a defect, pointed out clearly by Wallace Wohlking of Cornell University,* that is, it tries to change attitudes directly. Wohlking labeled this effort *TAB*:

T—*Train* people, especially supervisors, communicate with them, hold meetings, discussion groups, so that:

A—*Attitudes* will change—the supervisor's attitudes toward employees, the employees' attitude toward the organization—so that:

B—*Behavior* of the employees will then improve, along with productivity and quality.

The evidence is pretty scant that this approach to changing employee attitudes does much more than cost money. Why not try to change behavior directly, and let the attitude change itself? Wohlking labeled this more helpful approach *SBA*:

S—Change the *situation* in which the employees are working. If productivity, quality, or results are bad, redesign the work flow, change the modules of work, the size of the cycle, the variety of task and skill; change the level of control; improve the feedback system, so that:

B—*Behavior* changes; the work is done differently now,

*"Attitude Change, Behavior Change," *California Management Review*, Winter 1970, pp. 45–47.

and it is more productive, or it is easier to do the work
this way, so that:

A—*Attitude* toward the work, toward the boss, toward the
whole organization changes without any effort to directly manipulate attitude.

In trying to bring about improvements in the workplace, the recommendation, then, is to avoid trying to
change attitudes directly—the *TAB* approach. Start talking first with the supervisors about the possibility of redesigning the flow of work, its control, and its feedback. Cite
the evidence of success; admit to some failures also (some
of my 19 original published studies were not successful).
Perhaps this can be labeled *training,* but its purpose is
not to change attitudes as much as it is to precipitate a
new or different *situation.* Let the supervisors remain
skeptical if they wish, but ask that they try something
different in the workplace.

Encourage the supervisors to work with their employees, in turn, not to change attitudes but to get ideas for
what might be done differently in the workplace and to
ascertain their willingness to go along with the changes.
Use green-lighting to ease the communication flow, but
encourage supervisors and employees to go beyond that,
to the stage where they are considering improvements in
the entire work process and task organization. Go
analytic.

These raw ideas can be the material the key person and
supervisors work with. It is at this stage that careful
thinking and planning starts. Consider the following:

1. What is going to be done to change the work situation? Are job assignments functionally complete and
   consistent? Perhaps only control and feedback need to
   be changed, but usually all three change.
2. What are the implementation steps that need to be
   taken, in what order?
3. What training, if any, must be undertaken? What, if

anything, should be published in company newspapers or magazines? Who should be asked to come to what meetings, for what purpose?

When these questions have been answered, when you have gone as far as you can toward involving the employees in the planning, you are well on the way to meeting Myers' dictum, "When people feel they belong to an organization, they tend to support its systems." To paraphrase Fred Herzberg, employees are saying, "Use me well, don't merely treat me well."* In this section we have emphasized the modern view that the best avenue toward bringing about this change is to start using employees well; their attitudes will take care of themselves.

---

*See, for example, Herzberg's concluding note in "One More Time: How Do You Motivate Employees?" *Harvard Business Review,* January–February, 1968, p. 62.

6

maintaining the motivation

CHAPTER 5 DEALT WITH STARTING a job redesign effort somewhere in the organization. This chapter deals with keeping the project alive. It is my belief that the natural course of a job redesign effort is for it to start, flourish, and then die. Although the concepts of job redesign are not difficult, execution of a redesign project is. There are many natural forces working against survival of the project. On two occasions I asked groups of key people to name these forces. Here is a list of problems they had faced in getting job redesign efforts started:

Boss Problems
1. The boss (or the boss's boss) wouldn't risk a new procedure.
2. The boss believed a key, higher boss had not put job redesign on the list of priorities; other things intervened and nothing further was said.
3. The boss really did not learn what had to be done at the workshop conference.
4. The boss accepted the idea, but delegated the task to subordinates.
5. The boss believed in the project, rated himself as an advocate of Theory Y (workers are dependable and

self-motivated) but claimed that topside was Theory X (workers are undependable and lazy) in its orientation ("Let's get the work out even if we have to knock a few heads together").

6. Topside really was Theory X in orientation, and it had not been oriented to bad job design as a problem.
7. No one had worked out the true costs of goofing off, absenteeism, tardiness, quitting, retraining, and job inexperience, all of which might be traceable to poorly designed jobs.

General Fears

8. What will the unions do to us?
9. Things could be worse; better leave things alone.
10. Has this been tried at headquarters yet? They won't back us.
11. Try it on a less critical group than my people; how about our cafeteria workers?
12. If this is successful, we'll have to raise wages.
13. Our entire job structure setup will become obsolete if people have a larger scope to their jobs.
14. There's nothing left to redesign; the job is almost completely mechanized now.
15. This is too good to be true; you all will go away and that will be the end of it; we've been through these programs before.
16. You're just raising false expectations for the employees and for us bosses.
17. Let's take a survey instead; we could ask them if they want their jobs redesigned.
18. Our employees just want to get the hell out of here at night, especially on Fridays; they're not interested in this.

To keep redesign projects alive, key people (managers or people specifically assigned to the task) must be able to manage themselves and this natural inertia.

I would add another observation from my own experience as to where reluctance to go ahead may concentrate. It's at the middle management levels, especially in large organizations where middle management is out of contact with daily problems on the work floors. Top management, by which I mean the chairperson, president, and the "cabinet" of officers, generally supports the aims of good job design and wants something done.

Likewise, the two lowest levels of supervision usually like the redesign effort and fall in love with it as interpersonal tensions start to decrease in the workplace. I will even risk saying that if a mini-group is part of the redesign, its supervisors will be especially in love with the concept. Hesitation is most likely to be found at the third and fourth levels, or those levels where the bosses are more removed from the people and the needs of the workplace, but are extremely sensitive to pressure from above. Middle management knows there will be trouble from topside should productivity, quality, or service fall into even temporary disarray as the redesign effort gets under way. Any geographical isolation or distance between these three groups aggravates the problem of lower management versus middle management versus headquarters. And if middle managers' existing operating results are not very good, count on them to be especially sensitive to any further declines, even temporary ones.

Clearly, there is a lot going against the key person's efforts at job redesign. The tide of habit carries the organization the other way. Therefore, the following tested ideas for countering this natural tendency merit close attention.

1. *The prime lesson: Have a key person.* If job redesign projects are not actively pursued by key people from the day they run the original workshops through the various phases of follow-up, the odds are quite high (maybe 10 to 1) that the effort will die an early death. Job redesign is harder to accomplish than it appears to be. Managers will fail to take the steps, employee by employee, that will eventually release them for the truly managerial tasks of

their position. Instead they will continue to act at the first level of management like the "chief-est" of the clerks, the chief test person, chief operator, chief wirer—the best performer of the bunch. The job of the key person is to see that the redesign project is not neglected.

It is always inconvenient and a little frightening to make changes, especially changes in the direction of the unknown. It seems that our natural tendency is to avoid change. And so one may hope that it won't be necessary to start a job redesign effort at all if the employment office starts sending better people, or the new training facility turns out better products, or if we get a better grade of person when we move our new quarters out to Wonderfultown, or if the new administration in Washington takes the heat out of the economy, or puts some in.

The job of the key person is to help people make, and adjust to, changes by going back every two or three weeks and counseling the supervisors, singly or in groups: "How are you coming along? What responsibilities have you given to which employees? Could we go over the 'name vs. item' grid together? What did that employee say? Is anyone saying anything?" Encourage the family of supervisors responsible for the project to have a can-you-top-this session in which they report signs of progress. Of course, the supervisors should also talk freely about any difficulties or doubts they have. Then build from there; get agreement from the manager or the group on what comes next. Visits less than two weeks apart are likely to seem like badgering, and visits more than three weeks apart may seem like abandonment.

In sum, the first item in a prescription for the successful pursuit of a job redesign effort is to *have a key person.* The key person's first job is to get the redesign project started; thereafter, the key person's job is to keep the project going.

2. *Four rules to govern the game.* These rules will help you keep the job redesign effort from needlessly running afoul of other people.

Rule 1: No speed-ups. No change should be instituted that is actually a "speed-up" in sheep's clothing. Items for change that cause people to work smarter will be appreciated. But people should not be asked to work harder or faster.

Rule 2: No layoffs and no firings. As a result of an increase in productivity or other improvements there may be excess personnel. Such excess-personnel problems need to be handled, of course—but not by firing. For example, people, both management and nonmanagement, who were no longer needed in various directory compilation locations were either reassigned laterally, promoted, or simply not replaced as normal attrition occurred. Be prepared to reassign employees who are no longer needed when their jobs have been redesigned.

Rule 3: No poaching. No employee or mini-group should steal work usually assigned to other people. If an obvious deficiency in design exists, whose elimination would result in the destruction of certain jobs, include the people holding those jobs in the project once this has been discovered. Then the "no layoff" rule applies to the combined group.

Rule 4: No hurting the organization. No change that improves the job of an employee or a mini-group should be tolerated if it hurts the total organization, either financially, in its public image, or in its relation to its customers.

In short, part of the prescription for success is: Don't tolerate job changes in the name of good job design that will hurt the individual employee, other employees, the customers, or the organization as a whole.

3. *Have a definite plan and philosophy of when and how you will involve rank-and-file employees.* Someone in the organization is bound to offer job participation, worker democracy, and similar humane ideas, either as shortcuts to the redesign of good jobs or as the "right" course to follow even if it results in the involvement of too many

people for too many days. The following approach is offered from my experience with rank-and-file job redesigning even though some people felt that the approach was not democratic enough. Key people should face up to the issue of rank-and-file involvement if they want the effort to succeed.

Stage I: Present the concepts and involve supervisors and upper management only; don't involve rank and file until you know whether a project is possible.

Stage II: Encourage supervisors to participate with their employees in the actual redesign of jobs. Here we prefer short "deskside" work meetings (see point # 17 later in this section) rather than formal meetings and presentations. This puts the burden for initiating items of change and actually handling the change upon the supervisors where it belongs.

Stage III: Encourage employees to participate in turn with customers/clients/tasks. Seek additional feedback and ideas for improvement from them.

This "take it easy" approach to the participation of everyone concerned has these merits: (1) It saves time. Bosses can be converted more quickly if they have a chance to express ideas and opinions in a sheltered situation, away from the work floor where there may be many ancient angers still on hand. (2) It avoids confrontation. Bosses have a chance to lay a plan for change that will almost surely call for a great deal of communication skill on their part with such groups as employees, union stewards, customers, clients, or members of other departments. (3) It saves face for the bosses. If some of their pet procedures have to go, the efforts will probably move faster if the bosses are allowed to dispose of them personally. (4) It avoids bargaining, with unions or without unions, about what the distribution of eggs from the golden goose will be, until it is learned whether there will be any eggs.

In short, the eventual goal is disclosure to all levels of employees—no exceptions. But if a group of supervisors decides not to go ahead with a job design and work organization effort at a certain time and place, this wish must be respected. Premature insistence on participation by these supervisors and their workers can be damaging. This part of the key person's job—aiding supervisory groups to move ahead in a helpful way with the people reporting to them—demands tact and kindness.

4. *It is a special case of worker participation when the employees themselves raise the question of redesigning their jobs.* In effect, they initiate the effort and not their bosses. This happened in the headquarters example discussed in Chapter 5. The bosses concurred in a redesign effort and the entire work group met together. We quickly learned that the theory and ideas of job design could be projected to all at once, but that the meetings moved faster and without hostility if the bosses went to Room A and the workers went to Room B when the time came to actually draw up a list of ideas for redesigning the job. Open discussion of specific procedures that need to be changed can arouse anger and defensiveness. When the lists of ideas are worked out separately by the bosses and the bossed, and each group presents its ideas through a selected spokesperson, we have repeatedly seen bosses and bossed comment upon, and even laugh aloud at, the similarity of the lists. A smaller task force can then be appointed, charged with reaching decisions as to a future course, and the redesign project has begun. Frequently the task force includes both bosses and the bossed.

If and when the strategy calls for a joint meeting of bosses and bossed, consider using this tested formula: (1) The ideas and theories of job redesign, the case studies and films (if any) can be presented jointly. (2) The bosses and the bossed should, separately, develop lists of what can and should be done. (3) The lists should be compared in joint session. Special note: Let the bosses present their proposals first. Almost everything on their list will appear on the list of the bossed, which will make it far easier to get a task force appointed for action. On the one occasion where we had the bossed start the presentation of ideas for changes in their jobs, the bosses were so defensive that we wondered whether the employees would be able to finish their list. The whole time the bosses were saying uneasily, "Yes, we know. We have that on our list also. Just go ahead."

5. *The key person's responsibility is to improve the quality of jobs.* The key person should help supervisors clean up the maintenance items that need changing (light, heat, seats, parking lot, cafeteria, rest rooms, smoking, company policies, vacations, etc.). But this is not the work itself, and the key person must help supervisors sense the difference. If employees get a lift in morale from these changes, all well and good. "Now, let's get back to our effort, which is concerned with the design of the work itself, not the surrounding items." A newly improved, secure parking lot caused one employee to say, "Now I have a nice place to park before I come in to do my dum-dum job."

Maintenance items and the jobs themselves are separate matters. In contacts with employees, the key person listens to maintenance and job issues and if possible does something about both. But the key person's responsibility is for job quality. Insist that the work motivators (module/feedback/control) be given priority over maintenance needs. Get started on the basic job changes, and let changes in the maintenance items come somewhat later. No fanfare should accompany them either, such as "As a result of our job redesign effort, we are going to institute a monthly newsletter!"

6. *The key person should help supervisors fend off any distracting management programs that come along for perhaps six months to a year.* Get back to headquarters, or the source of the new effort, and explain that a job design or redesign project is under way, that it calls for no diversions for a while. In active organizations, it isn't pos-

sible to completely encapsulate a project area, but the key person may be able to fend off some diversionary programs. (Note that Red Cross drives, United Way appeals, antilitter campaigns, etc., are not "how to manage" programs and are not under discussion here. They can be pursued as usual.)

7. *The key person needs to prevent publicity.* If an exciting new breakthrough occurs in the redesign of an older job, along with producing some good operating results, publicizing it can hurt the supervisors. Often the hurt will be felt by other management people in their own divisions who are being bypassed in the publicity, and who may have rather good operating results of their own, obtained in other ways. If "prevent" seems too strong a notion, consider at least controlling the kind and amount of attention, keeping it on the modest side and aimed at persons who need to know.

8. *Don't lead the organization to expect big improvements in a short time as a result of job redesign.* Sell the expectation of a slow buildup of improvements through: (1) improved productivity or quality of service, (2) better employee attitudes, (3) better customer/client attitudes, (4) greater ease among managers in operating their departments. Sooner or later, differences will be noticeable. If your efforts are to be viewed as successful, you must have some standards of your own, at the start, as to what amount of change will be an acceptable minimum. *No change* in any of the four areas specified won't be satisfactory. But slow change in any one or more of them may be a good beginning.

9. *Help the department get the attention of management when there are good results and tested new procedures that deserve dissemination.* To keep this part of the effort moving smoothly, try to start with top management so as to avoid possible cross-currents while you enlist support for further presentations down the line.

By disseminating good results properly, honestly, and adequately, and explaining how they were obtained, the key person soon has other customers/clients/tasks. If results look promising and reasonable, others will want help also. You will soon have more work than you can handle. These new projects will help you counter your natural tendency to "help your first project to death." Instead, you can schedule yourself out the door. By now the group you are working with should have grown of its own a few key people who can carry the project forward. Rest assured that you will continue to have work, that your ability to do this innovative job, to see an emergency situation as a chance to make even better jobs for people, will still be sought after, even though the organization is developing key people of its own.

10. *Expect every group you work with to generate its own ideas.* Don't let new groups passively accept plans laid by other groups. Remember, we are trying to "light a fire" that will enable managers to continue the design of good jobs as new problems face a group of employees. We want managers to know the principles involved. After years of experience and hundreds of hours spent in various management training courses, I have concluded that this approach to job design through a family of supervisors is as powerful a management training "course" as I have ever seen. It is "hands-on" management training; the family of supervisors can make changes as soon as they wish.

11. *Concentrate on existing jobs first, even those that are very old.* They may be the ones most in need of redesign. New jobs will be easier to design thanks to the experience gained through working on existing jobs and to the help of supervisors with whom you have worked. They will even tell you of jobs in the dreaming-up stage, jobs you might otherwise not hear about until much later.

12. *Work on jobs in the mainstream of the business or organization.* These are the jobs that make a difference to the organization's success. Don't be diverted into first trying out these ideas on some safe jobs, such as cafeteria workers, supply room people, the security force. Bet on where the big payoff will be—on the mainstream jobs.

13. *Don't hesitate to work on the jobs of the lowest levels of supervisors first of all.* At one time I recommended working on craft and clerical jobs first, moving then to the jobs of the supervisors. Experience has shown me that often nothing can be done for craft- or clerical-level jobs until something has been done for the first-level supervisors. In fact, to improve certain supervisors' jobs, we had to push many responsibilities downward to the craft-level people that over the years had crept up to the bosses' level. When supervisors were freed of what they viewed as petty details and endless paper work, and when they knew the theory and actual practice of good job design, they carried the ideas to the craft-level jobs without any special meetings or green-light sessions; they did it informally, and successfully.

Just which management level is the lowest, the one that should receive immediate attention, can be a puzzle in a large organization. For example, with respect to the headquarters, middle management jobs discussed in Chapter 5 in the section on helping managers redesign their own jobs, we should note that those jobs, representing headquarters' desires and wishes to field organizations, were essentially basic jobs, workers' jobs rather than managers' jobs. Usually these managers had no one reporting to them.

My revised suggestion is to work on any job so basic that failure to fix it will mean that nothing else will be improved anywhere. For example, if the first-level supervisors' jobs are greatly in need of attention, they will do nothing for their employees until their own jobs are fixed. In effect, they would become gatekeepers to the whole situation. Changing craft and clerical jobs always results in changes in the jobs of the supervisors. Although this may be a direct approach to improving both jobs, it will not succeed if the supervisors won't cooperate.

14. *Concentrate first on groups where the management team will probably remain reasonably intact during the implementation stage.* New supervisors may be sympa-

thetic to the concepts, but they will have many other immediate adjustment problems on their minds. Job redesign is a long-range effort. Wait until new members of an organization have settled into their jobs before approaching them. If they approach you, that's different; then it may be an ideal time for significant changes.

15. *Be willing to tackle any job.* Don't decide in advance that a job is hopeless or that it is okay as is. Even if a job does not require much change, the workshop held to redesign it will earn you and your effort many friends.

16. *Do not drop any current procedures, controls, or restrictions on a job until you have prepared specific substitutes or alternative courses.* This item came forcibly to my attention when a sensitive, though rather strict, supervisor remarked, "Well, if they want us to let the employees run this place, I guess it will have to be okay with me." Job redesign does not mean job abandonment. Help supervisors to plan a shift in procedures, but not to abandon their employees or to feel abandoned themselves.

17. *In general, recommend that supervisors make changes selectively with employees, one at a time as they seem to want more responsibility or challenge.* This we call a "deskside" approach (in contrast with the "broadside" approach of instituting changes all at once, which is appropriate for job changes that will affect everyone). This is not a violation of the American credo that everyone must be treated alike. Everyone eventually becomes a candidate to receive all the rights, responsibilities, and job privileges that others have. Some are beginners, new to the job. In due season they have become experienced workers, receiving greater responsibilities and privileges.

18. *Encourage adoption of the "pro" concept.* First laid out in the Bell System by my colleague Malcolm Gillette, this concept bears on the issues of employee participation and equal treatment. Gillette and the key people in one of our outstandingly successful projects believed in the need to recognize that in a huge organization some employees

are beginners, learning the rudiments of a job. And beginners have plenty to do, without any fancy talk about redesigning the job. A good job design can take this into account, but too often the design falls short in that the job is appropriate only to the needs and abilities of new people. The "pro" (short for "professional") knows the initial job thoroughly and is ready to go well beyond that. Why not continue to transfer rights, privileges, and responsibilities to any employee who achieves well, until there are no more "rights" to give and the employee has the "ultimate assignment." Clearly, this is a person-by-person achievement, and affords a way of tailoring the job to the individual. This longitudinal concept of job design appears to me to be the very pinnacle of employee participation. It says in essence, "You can do as much as you want to do, go as far as you can go. How far do you want to go? Are you ready for another step?"

Here is an example of the "pro" concept in action. Five switchboard operators had to be assigned to an overflow switchboard, one used only in periods of high toll-calling (for example, during peak business hours, emergencies, Christmas time). On one particular day there was no supervisor available for the small group. Moreover, one supervisor for only five people was too heavy a management/worker ratio, anyhow. A key person suggested that a supervisor might not be needed if pros only were invited to work at the overflow positions. Management agreed to this, and five pros were asked, one at a time, if they would like to work the overflow switchboard and supervise themselves. Essentially this was a pro item no one had even dreamed of early in the project. In effect, the ultimate assignment was "ultimate, plus one."

All five operators accepted. As the days went along, the toll-call registers indicated that these positions were quite productive as a whole (individual registers were not available, but the total count of the number of calls going through the board was known). The pros were happy, and the company was saving the cost of a supervisor. A supervisor from the main floor made occasional, *scheduled and announced* trips to the overflow board to relieve people and to talk about current problems or work assignments for the coming days. Eventually, many pros were assigned to other boards in the building where the supervision was also minimal.

Some of the lessons the key people learned from this experience are:

—There is practically no end to what can be done with a job, depending upon time of year, special situations, emergencies, etc. There will always be something coming along to challenge a pro if the job is designed well.

—The important ingredient is the point of view of the supervisors toward their people, their pros.

—Job redesign takes time; about a year elapsed from the first sessions with supervisors to the overflow board situation.

—The key person's job is to visit, to help solve problems, to talk to other departments or to headquarters staff so that new procedures are legitimized.

—The unions loved this situation because of the mature way pros were treated. (The question of extra pay for the pros, which is frequently raised by outsiders, is actually irrelevant here, and everyone involved knew it. The operators' wages are bargained nationally and depend upon service (tenure), the hours worked, the shift involved, holidays, weekend work, overtime, and so on. No extra pay is offered or expected.)

—The unions, supervisors, everyone agreed that no employees had to be pros if they did not want to be. This is the kind of "employee participation" to which I am deeply committed.

—Finally, although not every employee performed well in the unsupervised situation, this was not viewed as a reason to deny the added responsibility to everyone. The pro concept, with its "ultimate assignment," is a successful one.

19. *Encourage supervisors to give responsibilities to employees even if there is some doubt as to their readiness.* There may be a testing period between boss and employees while the employees decide whether the redesign effort is real or merely a clever management game. And there will be errors; not all employees want or can manage greater responsibilities. A deskside approach, by the way, will make it easier for both manager and employee to beat a retreat than will a broadside approach.

The concept of "readiness" is elusive. In one case, a union stewardess was asked if she would like to make certain tallies of the amount of work she accomplished and keep her own chart. "No," she said. "That's the job of the service assistant [a higher-ranking job]. Let her do it." The supervisor beat a retreat in this instance. However, other people in the same group accepted the offer and started keeping their own charts, freeing themselves from monitoring by the higher-ranked people. In a few months, the stewardess indicated that she would prefer to keep her own production tally also, and the supervisor gracefully agreed to this.

20. *Arrange for and place faith in individual feedback systems for learning about one's performance and results.* Favor feedback plans that pit employees against their own previous performance rather than against other employees. Employees will almost surely call their good results to each other's attention, which is quite all right and can even be good fun. But the supervisors should be encouraged to stay out of that kind of rivalry. Competition has been used a great deal and is sometimes effective for short-term gains, but is usually ineffective as a long-range motivator. Pitting employees against each other usually calls for prizes, trophies, and rewards, all costly and of dubious merit. Prefer a feedback system that the individual can affect, one that will accurately reflect changes in performance. Train employees in how to control results. Let them post their own results on charts or forms which they keep. Let them set goals while

you contribute your ideas and take an interest in their results. Start betting on individual motivation rather than on group pressure.

21. *Assume that supervisors will need help and constant encouragement in the long task of job improvement.* The theory is easy; the practice is difficult. Encourage supervisors to swap experiences in monthly meetings in which they share experiences, both good and bad. In the best approach that I witnessed, the big boss of an entire area, with 3,600 employees in many departments, scheduled quarterly meetings, beginning at 9 A.M. and continuing through lunch, for all middle management people and selected supervisors and a few of their rank-and-file employees. The only subject of discussion was their experiences in the design or redesign of jobs, with recommendations for particular approaches and reasons for following them.

Managers would present their supervisors to the audience, who in turn presented employees who were working under new job designs. A friendly question-and-answer period would take place between the employees, their supervisors, and the middle managers as to how things had been, how they were now, how they all felt about it. Sometimes other members of the audience would call for clarification. This was not an easy experience, especially for young or new employees. Yet the meeting went so well and so naturally that a number of participants were chosen to appear on an NBC-TV documentary called "Humanizing Work" and hosted by Edwin Newman. Employees were interviewed informally at their actual work locations rather than at the quarterly conference, but the accounts described at the conference were the reason for their being selected to participate in the TV program. These quarterly conferences on the design of jobs were extremely stimulating to *other* supervisors, even those from different departments.

As indicated earlier (item no. 7), excess publicity eventually becomes a problem, especially after a few top officers from the parent company reported very favorably upon what they had seen and heard in a quarterly meeting the day they slipped into the audience unannounced, just as the employees began to talk about their jobs, before and after redesign. Nevertheless, and despite some risks, the idea of planned meetings where management people can share experiences is strongly recommended. This is the surest way for supervisors at remote locations to learn how the big bosses view the matter.

The key person, in this case, prepared the agenda very carefully, based upon reports he was receiving from locations where significant changes and results were occurring. Soon others in line management jobs were acting as key people, cooperating in the spread of the concepts and the practice of job design through workshops, as prescribed in item no. 13. Before long, these additional key people, usually at middle management level, were scheduling employees from their own divisions to represent them at the quarterly conference. The strength of this successful program lay in the planning for additional key people from among the actual line managers, who took over the responsibilities of the one, staff key person, who eventually moved on to other assignments.

22. *Expect supervisors to go forward on their own to redesigning other jobs once they have worked through one redesign situation with you.* At first, use selected supervisors as associate key people to help you run workshops and green-light sessions and to follow through on progress. Then turn the major responsibility for a meeting over to them. Gradually, these selected people become their own key people. Keep your own staff very small; remember the rule in item no. 2: Don't steal other people's work.

23. *Train higher levels of management to ask repeatedly about the job design program.* "How is the job design effort going? What can I do to help? Does something need to be changed at my level?" If the quarterly conference or a substitute is not a possibility, this will be the next best procedure for keeping your effort going.

24. *Go multidepartmental if several departments ex-*

ist. That is, don't confine the job redesign effort to one department if you are invited elsewhere. Ask newly trained key people to help you. To improve jobs in one department, functions that lie elsewhere may have to be moved. If the other department is engaged in job redesign also, the chances for harmonious results are much greater. It is conceivable that a mini-group across departmental lines might be the best arrangement.

25. *Encourage supervisors to build ladders of jobs.* These are sets of jobs in the organization that competent and ambitious employees can move into one after the other—jobs that will provide them with challenging work for a long time. When employees have become pros and their current jobs can't be further enriched, the ladder of jobs permits continued growth and learning for employees without their having to scheme or dream about getting out of this organization in order to get ahead. This is a tough assignment for the supervisory family. The concept of "career pathing," as it is often called—letting competent employees move from one enriched job to another—is completely in harmony with the job design concepts presented in this book.

26. *Conduct exit interviews with people leaving the organization through resignation, reassignment, or rotation.* Encourage them to talk openly about why they're leaving and how they think their job could have been better. Actual tape recordings, made with consent, of course, have proved stimulating and helpful in the search for ideas to make jobs more attractive and in getting attention to a problem of poor job design. Watch for jobs characterized by rapid turnover.

27. *Be the conscience of the organization.* People deserve the best jobs we can give them, not only along traditional monetary and humane lines but also in the quality of their assignments. Many are hardened and cynical about their work. They won't believe this effort is "for real," that a corporation, an organization, really cares. Many managers, remote from headquarters, are equally

hard-bitten and disbelieving. They have lived through many campaigns where, to survive, they had to cheat a little, where the motivational technique used by headquarters was "threat," sometimes overt, sometimes covert, but always there. Now the motivational thrust being proposed from headquarters avoids threat and emphasizes job quality. "Hmm," says the manager, "very interesting—if it's true."

I remember well one employee saying in an exit interview, "One-third of my life, day after day, week after week, is spent at my job. All I ask is this, 'Please, God, don't let this be a waste of my life!'" You will find that employees at all levels of an organization will value you if you speak for them on this matter, address their concerns. So "hang in there"; even the cynics won't hate you.

Summary

The prescriptions in this chapter can be boiled down to 27 statements:

1. From the outset center responsibility for keeping the job design effort going in a key person.
2. Don't let a project hurt the employees; don't tolerate poaching of other people's jobs; don't tolerate layoffs or firings if the projects are successful; and don't let a project hurt the company or organization.
3. Let all employees participate, but in well-planned stages.
4. Encourage headquarters people, especially, to start projects if you want to set off a secondary wave through them reaching to the outer edges of the organization.
5. Give top priority to redesigning jobs, but be willing to help the organization make needed changes in maintenance items.
6. Fend off distracting management programs for a while.

7. Prevent publicity, or at least control it.
8. Don't sell the idea of big improvements in a short time; sell the idea of a long, slow pull upward.
9. Get the attention of top management when good results are at hand.
10. Expect every supervisory group to generate its own ideas for job redesign.
11. Concentrate on existing jobs first; supervisors will then know how to set up new jobs.
12. Work on jobs in the mainstream of the organization rather than on the "safe" jobs.
13. Start with key jobs that might unlock the doors to other jobs, such as the job of first-level supervisors.
14. Begin with work groups where the team of managers is likely to remain relatively intact for the period of the project.
15. Be willing to tackle any job.
16. Drop no current job procedures until a substitute is ready.
17. Prefer a "deskside" to a "broadside" approach in giving employees increased responsibilities.
18. Encourage the growth of a pro concept, wherein an employee obtains more and more control over the module and its feedback (an ultimate assignment).
19. Encourage supervisors to give employees new responsibilities, even if there is a doubt about their readiness.
20. Set up an individual feedback system; discourage group competition as a long-range motivator.
21. Plan carefully for meetings where supervisors will be encouraged in their efforts and will give and receive new ideas for job design.
22. Train management people to act as their own key people.
23. Train top management to ask repeatedly, "How is the job design effort going?"
24. Go multidepartmental if many departments exist and

changes in jobs in one department affect jobs in other departments.

25. Encourage the organization to build a ladder of good jobs, a career path, with the potential for motivating people for years.
26. Conduct exit interviews.
27. Be the conscience of the organization.

7

---

the quiet revolution

THE STORY BEHIND GOOD JOB DESIGN as a neglected road toward greater productivity and happiness started to break in the late 1960s. Since then, there has been some disappointment on the part of very decent people who want the effort to succeed. Things move too slowly. Measurable gains are hard to produce. Projects are not failing with really damaging, negative results, but the successes are not striking. But there were and are positive results, and, at least in my experience in the Bell System, top management truly *wanted* us to succeed. Repeatedly I was told, "Of course this is the right road to follow." As indicated in the last chapter, the corporate view was to get started, with the understanding that it would take time to get results. And the effort still moves ahead.

As one indicator, an excellent one-hour color film was prepared, for internal use only, on the training of supervisors. It uses documentary materials exclusively. No actors, no script, just people working at jobs—some before, some after the redesign of their jobs—and talking about their jobs. It is significant that the film is called "The Quiet Revolution." Great, majestic things don't happen, but little improvements are shown to add up. And in this final chapter of Part I, I want to review some of the implications of this quiet revolution, going far beyond the film.

The greatest revolution, the *first,* in the area of jobs, was the Industrial Revolution of the 1770s. Men and women came in from their fields and cottages to plants where costly machinery was driven by water, wood fires, and coal or other fossil fuels. No longer could cottagers compete with their handlooms or forges. Jobs were pretty bad, child labor was customary, but it was an inexorable step toward the plentiful supply of goods, foods, and services that we now enjoy.

A *second revolution* occurred about 100 years later (around the 1870s), with Frederick Taylor and the *scientific managers.* Uniform work procedures, timed and enforced by the stop watch, sprang to life. Identical parts that could be routinely assembled were the order of the day. The assembly jobs were pretty bad too. In addition, people were illiterate, poorly housed, and poorly fed.

That is no longer the situation. We are on the verge of a *third revolution,* again approximately 100 years after the last one. This time the behavioral scientists are calling to the attention of the industrial designers and engineers, and any other managers who lay out tasks for other people to perform, that there is an intelligent, educated human being inside those overalls, that dress, that Brooks Brothers suit, who must be used just as efficiently as the machines we use so well. Human beings who could do a lot more for a company than they do are not being used well.

If we start from this position—that most employees could do more for the organization than they do now and that faulty job design is at the root of the problem—then there are many implications for many of us that follow from it.

Implications for a Basic View of People

If employees perform poorly, it's a learning failure, not a case of innate moral infirmity. "People are no damn good" implies innate moral infirmity. Rather, we need to recognize that the goof-off person has learned this response to work situations.

Why have some employees learned to perform so poorly? Just as children can have difficulty learning to read and can develop negative attitudes toward reading because of unpleasant experiences when learning the skill, employees can develop negative attitudes toward work and learn to perform poorly. One cannot be ordered to be motivated to work, just as one cannot be ordered to want to read.

We are now quite certain that the well-informed manager or industrial engineer can arrange the content of single tasks and then groups of tasks so that they become more attractive, more motivating than other arrangements. The switch in thinking is a small one: from attempting to motivate employees externally to setting the conditions of work so that the employee is motivated by the task.

Using modern learning theory as a guide, certain consequences of thinking this way can be stated:

1. When employees fail to perform, this means in most cases that the manager does not have the tasks set right. Conventional wisdom finds fault with the employee. Occasionally this is correct. But we must ask why there is an annual force loss of 30 to 40 percent on some jobs, while on other similar jobs in similar locations and with similar pay and benefits the annual loss may be only 10 to 20 percent. The analysis of this question will not be easy. In the high-turnover situation, it is possible that the task itself is hopeless or that management has not maximized its attractiveness. We must examine the different assumptions managers make and differences in the way people are used, since differences in pay or external conditions are ruled out as explanation.

We have said that people *learn* the motivation to work. If many people act irresponsibly at work, if they act in Theory X fashion, as Douglas McGregor called it, it seems reasonable to say that irresponsible behavior is the natural reaction in the work situation. It's learned behavior, learned in that situation. On this note, Henry Ford's view is relevant: that the average worker wants a job in which he does not have to put forth much physical effort—and, above all, in which he does not have to think. The Detroit assembly line was perfected in an effort to meet both needs as Henry Ford saw them. How then can we complain if the worker does unthinking things!

This view of auto workers, which prevailed in 1922, still exists today. "Edward N. Cole, the president of General Motors, said at a news conference in San Francisco [in 1972] that G.M. workers actually preferred repetitive work. He said that the workers felt they were under less pressure, did not have to think about the jobs and could let their minds wander to think about more important things."*

2. The highly fragmented production line breeds worker irresponsibility. Worker irresponsibility did not breed the production line. Such lines depend not only on machine power but also on the fact that people can be programmed to perform the pieces of work that don't fit well into complete automation.

A quotation from Joseph Godfrey, head of General Motors Assembly Division, in *Automotive News* reveals that Godfrey thinks of human beings as though they were machines that must not be thrown out of rhythm: "The workers may complain about monotony, but years spent in the factories leads me to believe that they like to do their jobs automatically. If you interject new things, you spoil the rhythm of the job, and work gets fouled up." †

When a machine breaks down, we do not contend that the machine is irresponsible; that would merely divert us in our search for the trouble. Similarly, to characterize workers as irresponsible when they fail in their machine-like jobs is to miss the issue. The fact is that people are

*The New York Times, September 3, 1972.
†Quoted by Geoffrey Norman, "Blue-Collar Saboteurs," *Playboy,* November 1972, p. 251.

poor machines, a fact neglected by the designers of the traditional production line.

3. Union leaders do not accept the view that people are machines. For example, they agreed with leaders of the automobile industry in the nationally approved 1973 labor contract to share equally in certain expenses connected with experiments that would more fully utilize the talents of workers. As indicated by the following few paragraphs from a speech by Irving Bluestone, vice president of the United Auto Workers, union leaders believe that employees eventually must have considerably more to say about the design and organization of their work if such mounting problems as absenteeism, labor turnover, drug and alcohol abuse, and poor quality levels are to be avoided.

Today we hear the terms "job enrichment," "job enlargement," "job rotation," "blue collar blues," etc. In personnel circles these are much-discussed issues, and perhaps in the first flush of new discovery there is being generated as much heat as light. In the broader sense, however, improving the quality of worklife relates to the ultimate fulfillment of industrial democracy. It is not simply a matter of "enriching," "enlarging," or "rotating" jobs. It is giving workers a participative role in managing their jobs and ultimately even a participative role in managing certain aspects of the enterprise. Democratizing industrial life is the key element in improving the quality of worklife. The historic management approach to life in the plant, which still relies largely on the implementation of "scientific management," is antagonistic to enhancing the dignity of the individual, without which the principles of democracy have no meaning. . . .

Worker participation in decision making should result in a departure from the miniaturization and simplification of the job to a system which embraces broader distribution of authority, increasing rather than diminishing responsibility and accountability, combined with the engineering of more interesting jobs, with the opportunity to exercise a meaningful measure of autonomy and to utilize more varied skills. It requires affording the worker every opportunity to exercise his creative and innovative ingenuity to the maximum extent of his capabilities. . . .

While wages and job security are indeed very important, the value which the individual worker may bring to the workplace, the opportunity to control the job instead of being controlled by it, the sense of self-fulfillment as part of work performance are vital aspects of worklife. And fulfillment of these desires is largely feasible. . . .

The worker entering the work force today holds a different view of society and the world in many respects than did his counterpart of a generation ago. Those entering the work force in the next generation will likewise reflect a different view as societal and cultural changes continue to occur.*

Repeatedly in recent years (my earliest newspaper clipping dates back to September 1973), Douglas A. Fraser, president of the United Auto Workers, has said that the union plans to make job monotony a bargaining issue. Current levels of wages in other industries, foreign competition, and the marketplace in general put limits on how much money workers can get, says Fraser, so the union might as well go after another high-priority item—the general quality of life for the person on the production line. Just how the two parties—labor and management—can bargain on this issue is not clear yet. When it does get figured out, it won't be just the auto workers who will bargain over the issue of job monotony.

4. Somewhere between no specialization of labor and great fragmentation lies a much better work setup as far as today's employee is concerned. We need not linger over rightness of thinking on the part of Frederick W. Taylor, Gantt, the Gilbreths, and other early advocates of scientific management. They did their work in an era of high immigration, poor food, poor medicine, low literacy, low technology, and no behavioral science research.

*"Decision Making by Workers," *The Personnel Administrator,* July–August 1974, pp. 26–30.

The evidence from the Bell System studies and a growing number of other companies indicates that many, though by no means all, employees will do much more, be more responsible, on their jobs if given the opportunity. That is, they will perform as in the assumption made by Douglas McGregor in his famous Theory Y. Even today there is much dispute over whether workers are undependable and lazy (Theory X) or dependable and self-motivated (Theory Y). The answer seems clear: Workers have the capacity to be either. The question is: Which do we want to develop and how do we do it?

5. Prior to the job design effort, the jobs that employees held were not viewed as causing poor employee performance. It is as though jobs were a constant. A customary objective of early industrial psychologists, in fact, was to measure employees and then fit them properly to the job. Testing became a fine art; the writing of job specifications became *de rigueur.* "We have the job and we have the test; start the employment line through, please." Current problems with force loss have made it clear that in the long run, this is not a good way to match jobs and people.

Warren G. Bennis, whose valuable and oft-quoted "Revisionist Theory of Leadership" reviews much of the literature on the job design effort, sees a group of workers as becoming either Theory X or Theory Y, depending on their job. But Bennis did not go all the way in his 1961 piece. He did not directly challenge the nature of the tasks that the organization gives, or suggest the tasks be made an experimental variable. To him, workers are variable, but not tasks or jobs. Bennis sees leadership as the problem. He holds that *"effective leadership depends primarily on mediating between the individual and the organization in such a way that both can obtain maximum satisfaction."** (Emphasis Bennis's)

Ten years later it appears that one major reason for the constant need to mediate between the individual and the

*"Revisionist Theory of Leadership," *Harvard Business Review,* January–February 1961, pp. 26ff.

organization is that the leader lacks information about other ways jobs might be arranged to yield greater satisfaction. The organization's goals (providing goods or services) are not likely to be the individual's goals (economic security and a meaningful work life). We in the job design effort ask: How can we vary the individuals' jobs so that their goals are met more frequently and for longer periods? The issue is not mediating skill but job quality.

Implications for Employees

Although the supporting evidence is still coming in, the job redesign approach is likely to have the following implications for employee performance and attitude, all of which are viewed as desirable by most employers:

1. Employees will stay longer on any one job, because job interest and force retention are directly related. I don't think we should expect new employees to stay, happily, in the job until age 60, but it might be nice if they stayed 60 months, or even 60 weeks.

2. If the jobs are optimally related (nested, minigrouped; not pooled), employees will stay longer in an effort to move upward in the organization.

3. Employees can learn other desirable jobs in the minigroup without the expense of formal training, merely by observing and helping. They will also have an informed basis for *not* wanting certain other jobs, which is an advantage to both the employees and the company.

4. Performance will be better from the point of view of customer/client/task, and employees will enjoy the individual feedback, if the feedback system is arranged properly. They will again feel they are important parts of a meaningful cycle.

5. Friction between employees in different departments will be reduced if they are in mutually supportive groups. In one situation in which this was not the arrangement, a telephone lineman quite angrily told how he had to argue with someone in the engineering department that the

pole upon which he had been standing for 25 minutes was indeed there even if whoever-it-was could not find it on his engineering drawing. A lineman from another city where mini-groups had been formed shrugged his shoulders and said, "That can't happen to me. I have my own engineer. I'd just go in and see him."

Implications for Managers

The performance of telephone employees and of employees in many other industries in the days of yore was generally rated excellent. In an effort to recapture it, employee campaigns are frequently launched. Examples: ZD (Zero Defects), PPIP (Personal Pride in Performance), IT (I Try), and so forth. Results: very little, because the job base, the fundamental task, is left unchanged. Since the job design effort aims to change the base, and since it is almost invariably in the direction the jobs took in days of yore, before fragmentation of module/control/feedback, there are certain implications for managers:

1. Excellent performance will reappear in the organization.

2. Managers will spend much more time managing jobs and less time on "people problems." The latter will not disappear, however.

3. Managers will seldom find themselves doing the work of the subordinates—except in emergency or training situations.

4. Managers will run mini-groups (related tasks) rather than pools (identical jobs). Their concern will be combining optimal groups of tasks.

5. Managers will learn to view a growing need for *checking* as a warning signal that the work itself is getting out of hand, that it is not challenging someone properly, and that the first investigation should center on the work process.

6. Where employees have outgrown a job psychologically and the job cannot be enriched anymore, managers

will repot them or plan career ladders for them. Good bosses will not grieve over the loss of good employees, even if it is temporarily bad for production. Bosses will learn to take pride in the number of their people who move up.

7. Bosses will handle employees differently in the work assignments they give, either because they are different in their abilities or are at different points on a learning curve. Not all will be given the ultimate assignment (maximum self-control), and none will be given it the first day. Bosses will recognize that they are headed toward a "lowest common denominator" style of managing if they refuse to let good performers work independently simply because it has been found necessary to restrict the responsibilities of poorer performers. Oddly enough, managers will recognize that the only way to treat employees is to treat them unequally. The trite phrase, "People are different," will at last take on practical as well as ethical meaning.

8. Bosses will realize when they hear other managers talking about the use of money rewards, indexes, contests, praise campaigns that these are parts of a different motivational approach—external motivation—which is likely to have only short-term value.

9. Bosses may feel guilty about a successful job design effort for employees. In one form or another this thought has been stated by many, many supervisors: "Actually, it's my job that has been enriched."

Implications for Design Engineers

Early in these attempts to enrich existing jobs, I became aware of some jobs that could not be improved, usually because their scope was constrained by a piece of equipment; sometimes tending that piece of equipment was the whole job. Obviously, the job-quality effort is enormously dependent upon the talents and understanding of design engineers, whether they are designing equipment or systems. They must be knowledgeable about their work and empathetic toward other humans, concerned about human factors in a new and enlarged sense.

"Human factors" specialists already exist in many industries and laboratories, but they concern themselves only with the physical part of the job. In Europe, they are called ergonomists; in the United States, biotechnicians or human factors specialists. In any case, their speciality is relating worker and work in an optimal way. They are likely to be well acquainted with the fields of physiology, sensory psychology, and anthropometrics. They try to answer the *can-do* question: Can an employee operate this piece of equipment? If not, how shall we modify it? The question raised in these pages is a different one—not can-do but *will-do:* Will an employee operate this piece of equipment reasonably happily over long periods of time? If not, how shall we modify the equipment and the whole job setup?

As an example of the difference, consider the machines operated by long lines of workers in our post offices, where they sort mail by zip code. A conveyor belt presents the letter briefly, the employee punches buttons for the necessary digits of the zip code, and away the letter goes to the right mailbag. I'm told it is a difficult job because it's monotonous. The employees *can* do it; however, they do not *want* to do it. The question that should be raised by biotechnicians is: How can we avoid this zip code sorting operation entirely? Yes, the machine design will work; no, we must not accept it as a solution. It is *semi*automatic, and the *semi* part falls on these workers. The objective should be to go all the way toward automation or stand still until complete automation is possible. We do not need thousands of additional monotonous jobs, the by-products of automation. People are too smart to be happy with these jobs. As I see it, we have run out of dum-dum people to do our dum-dum jobs.

In my personal experience, human factors specialists

have been most receptive to this point of view. I believe they will be even more receptive as top management backs them up when they refuse to okay a *can-do* design on the grounds that the jobs thus created will be hard to manage. As I mentioned earlier, in the Bell System, teams of specialists now look at designs from the point of view of (1) efficiency, (2) manageability, and (3) humanity. The humanity aspect has got to be soft-pedaled in our hard-nosed business society, but the job can be done.

Some implications for design engineers are:

1. Design engineers will not be able to help until they are given some tested principles from this field as a guide. While such principles do not exist in refined form, this has not stopped me from making a trial run, to be found in Chapter 4, "What Motivates."

2. In design efforts calling for teams of specialists, the design engineer should insist that behavioral scientists help on this aspect of the problem. Even the informal interviewing of employees in the trial job situation should be done with professional attention and concern.

3. The development of two relatively new measures will eventually help design engineers in figuring out the tradeoffs between the costs of a design or system and the quality of a job from the employee's point of view. The first is a standardized "Reaction to Your Job" questionnaire. This device needs to become more common and should be used with employees in trial runs. I wonder if this was done when the zip code sorting machine was in its trial phase? Eventually this should yield a "Goodness of Jobs" scale analogous to the "Hardness of Minerals" scale. At the moment, we have no scale for rating jobs comparatively so that one might specify a score below which a new job would not be accepted. But the questionnaire technology for this exists.

The second measure is a "Force Loss Cost Accounting" procedure that shows the dollar cost of losing people because of poorly designed jobs. Roughly speaking, these cost elements are: (1) the cost of running replacement advertising; (2) in fact, the cost per employee of running the entire employment office; (3) the cost of training for that job; (4) the cost of underproductivity as the new employee builds up to the productivity level of the former employee; and (5) the cost of overstaffing because of expected high force loss.

Most businesses have little or no idea of what it costs when an employee quits after a short time on the job. The employment office—with its personnel, medical examinations, and so forth—is the least of these costs. In fact, some of the costs cannot be computed, such as the loss of customers who are treated poorly by new employees and interruption of older employees who try to help the beginner. When I point out that some businesses actually lose more than 100 percent of their people in a year, someone usually laughs and retorts: "How can you lose more employees than you have!" It's easy: by replacing people two or three times a year.

A quick way for a company to get a first estimate of force loss is to count the number of W-2 tax forms that must be mailed out in January each year. When I suggested this at one conference, a furniture manufacturer volunteered, "We just mailed them out last week. I have 500 employees, and we mailed out 1,645 W-2 forms." That means 1,145 forms went to people no longer on the payroll. The manufacturer went on to say that excessive force loss was a big problem in his business. Perhaps his industrial engineers are not alert to this leak in the financial budget. Such information needs to become routinely available, and the specific problem jobs must be tracked down. It is likely that some jobs in the furniture manufacturer's plant have almost no turnover, and that certain others are accounting for virtually all of it.

4. In specific cases, as in the design of the zip code sorting machine, design engineers will increasingly be labeled "the cause" if employee reaction to the quality of jobs is adverse, if force loss is high, and if productivity fails to meet predicted levels.

Implications for Top Management

Job design concepts are deceptively simple. However, there are some profound implications for top management:

1. Top management cannot avoid reaching a decision in the long run as to its view of human beings. If it believes that employees will by nature make as little effort as possible, do not want to think, must be coerced to work (the Theory X views quoted earlier from Henry Ford and Edward Cole of General Motors), very different corporate jobs and procedures spring to life than under the assumptions of Theory Y. An organization cannot escape having a model for motivation. If top management makes no effort to state its point of view, then it has done so anyhow, by default. The amount of control given employees at the moment, the size of the slice of work, the use or non-use of punishment to get results are all indicative of a philosophy of management.

2. Indexes, rewards, and measurement schemes whereby management "motivates" the "laggards" will be recognized as negative approaches to motivation. Positive approaches, wherein indexes and feedback are viewed as tools of analysis for the employee, will eventually take priority. Older schemes of motivating from the outside will be reserved for workers who cannot move to a self-motivated basis.

3. If the organization is set up by functions (for example, engineering, production, marketing, sales, service) that come together only at some distant headquarters rather than right where the customers/clients exist, top management will know that it's time for reanalysis. One of the supreme tasks of top management is to decide how the resources of the organization will be used. When employee knowledge and potential are recognized as poorly exploited resources, a change in either job designs or the organization of work can help start the ball rolling toward better utilization.

4. The corporate laboratory, if the organization has one, and its design engineers should be charged with the responsibility of working all the way through a new design or system to see that it will maximize self-motivation of employees. If top management purchases machines and systems on the open market, it will learn to demand that suppliers answer the same question: How will our people view this system or machinery? What will happen to their performance once the novelty has worn off?

5. Top management may eventually learn how to specify this aspect of equipment or systems design, just as it specifies other performance potentials before acceptance for use.

6. Switching to this basis will call for a massive learning effort, probably requiring 10 to 15 years. Classroom training won't do the job. All managers will have to go through a laboratory exercise of their own. Even so, a few reassignments of difficult bosses or early retirements may be necessary before the organization moves over completely to the new concepts.

7. Top management will enjoy getting off the constant diet of short-duration solutions to the motivation problem (Zero Defects Program, Two-Way Communications, Skip-Level Meetings, etc., etc.). The new basis will require much patience, but it will be quite rewarding as a way of dealing with most employees.

8. Top management will not have gotten off the old diet until its members have a consistent, verbalizable philosophy of work that enables them to spot proposals that will act at cross-purposes to the new basic philosophy. For example, a new control process that lets the top boss in an operation know where bad results are occurring before anyone lower in that organization knows about it will quickly be recognized as a potential mischief-maker, as a lethal information loop.

9. Most corporations hold that they operate with *equal* interests in meeting the needs of the customers, the shareholders, and the employees. The job design effort

implies that customers and shareholders will do better if the corporation concentrates more energy on meeting the psychological needs of employees. This can be accomplished largely by improving the quality of their work.

Implications for Management Trainers

Since I have spent most of my business years in management training and development, I feel free to state a few preferences:

1. I would spend a lot of time helping families of managers (those reporting to a common boss, who work together daily) understand the principles of job design and work organization. This fundamental course on human motivation I would call, simply, Basic Management Training. If jobs are right, many other interpersonal tensions and problems will go away.

2. But not all. So I would have follow-up courses on communication skills, behavior modeling for supervisors, management by objectives, and so forth. These would not be offered to supervisors until they had done all they could to get jobs and the organization of tasks in reasonably good shape. These courses would be tailored to fit the situation of the family, and the training would be done with family groups wherever possible.

3. I would tend to avoid training courses that do not have a measurable result of some kind.

Implications for Union–Management Relations

The following implications stem from contacts with officers at the national level of three very large American unions. Small meetings were held in which we reviewed the purpose and the results of the job improvement projects and exchanged viewpoints. These are not necessarily typical unions. On the other hand, they *do* exist:

1. As long as job design does not threaten the economic security of employees, it is viewed as an excellent effort

by these top-echelon officers. They believe the effort can add significantly to employee satisfaction if it is handled well.

2. The union *expects* to get more money with every contract negotiation. Its leaders see the job design approach as one that may help guarantee their success in this effort, for this approach has often led to real gains in employee productivity. If employees themselves don't become more productive, then their annual wage increment must be covered by stepped-up automation or other means of reducing the work force. Certainly, the sophisticated union leader is well aware that increments due solely to inflation do not help the workers.

3. A job design effort is usually accompanied by a drop in the number of grievances. Union officers like to see this drop very much indeed; they insist they do not enjoy handling grievances.

4. The top echelons say they can be of great assistance in introducing job redesign concepts for current jobs to new locations, or in introducing new equipment or systems that have been designed to further the employees' view of themselves as useful, responsible people. They have explicitly offered to help, to set up a joint effort regarding the quality of future jobs.

5. As with the organization's own management, the management of the unions must be brought along to believe in the job design effort. No doubt many stewards and others in the hierarchy won't believe, at first, that the organization is sincere in its effort to improve the quality of work.

6. It has been stated that with a little bit of luck, this area of union–management relations might turn out to be one of statesmanlike cooperation and planning. On many other issues, the traditional union–management stance is that of adversaries. In its 1973 contract with the major auto makers, the United Auto Workers actually agreed to pay half of all consultation costs in getting job redesign demonstration projects started.

An Ethical Implication

Finally, is this job design effort the right thing to do? That's the ethical question. I lay aside as unworthy of consideration any suggestion that this effort is mere corporate or organizational manipulation to take advantage of workers. Such efforts have occurred in the past and are always unethical. But what kind of ethics is involved here?

Readers of articles in the current press are likely to find mention of no less than five kinds of job "ethics." Max Weber in his famous treatise *The Protestant Ethic and the Spirit of Capitalism* clearly pointed to the firmly entrenched Protestant belief in the virtue of hard work, that people of sloth and idleness most certainly would not be found in heaven.

On the other hand, as this century matured, a Welfare Ethic was rising in the land. It holds that there is nothing wrong with accepting, without any hesitation or labor, any economic goods you can get your hands on legally in a nation that has plenty of everything.

But back to the first hand again. In the minds of the young the Protestant Ethic was yielding to the Work Ethic. Work is a valuable basis for organizing one's life, not necessarily as a step toward obtaining a place in heaven but as a way of getting material goods right now. Hard work and heaven are not keystones in this concept. Instead, work is the ethical means to such earthly ends as economic goods, services, and a meaningful work life. Work is the center of life for adherents of the Work Ethic.

Opposing this—and very recently—is a fourth ethic, the Leisure Ethic. Its proponents hold that life should not be spent in toil, but in leisure. Maximize leisure. Trade off work for leisure at every opportunity. Press for the shorter week, for the separation of work from the rest of one's life. Work is an intrusion on leisure: "Don't get 'hooked' on work."

Perhaps this job design effort will lead to a fifth ethic, a

Life Ethic, which holds that life is a balance of work and leisure. Its proponents will say: "Never discount work as a valuable, central core around which a meaningful life can be built." That work can actually provide this core is fortunate in view of the fact that 99 percent of us are not independently wealthy; we must work whether we like it or not. But when a reasonable degree of security is at hand, a variety of leisure activities may come in. In this ethic, life is viewed as richer because of its contrasts. Work and leisure are not viewed as either-or; both are good indeed. There is no need for thinking in terms of a 50-50 balance, either. Unlike the Puritans who worried for their slothful neighbors, the adherent of a Life Ethic would actually accept slothfulness as a reasonable part of the whole life: "How about a little sloth tonight!"

I have observed that people being introduced to the concept of work as an important life motivator are likely to go overboard and hold that if work is motivating, maintenance factors are *therefore* not important. In time most people resolve the work and maintenance issue: They synthesize the two into a Work Ethic.

But the Life Ethic goes beyond that. It's a blending of the Work Ethic and the Leisure Ethic, taking the positive elements of both and coming up with a philosophy of life that places equal importance and acceptance on obtaining satisfaction in both major modes in which people operate: work and leisure.

part II

about your
own job

8

---

how good is your job?

THE TITLE OF THIS CHAPTER may seem to suggest that only one question about your job needs to be answered. In fact, there are three questions:

> How good is the job itself?
> How good is your total work situation?
> How good is your life?

This chapter will enable you to take inventory on the first two questions. The next chapter will bear on the third question. Answering each question leads to the next. If the task is bad, the total work situation can't be acceptable, and this will lead to a feeling that life itself is not worthwhile.

How Good Is Your Job?

The first requirement is for you to analyze the task, the assignment at which you work. In the next chapter, we will discuss what to do about it, if anything. Check the blocks in Questionnaire I that represent your best judgment of your own working situation. If you spend your days principally running your home, farming, or in some other solo occupation rather than as part of an organization, try to interpret the questions to fit your own situation. We make no pretense as to precise measurement here—this is a set of questions designed to help you make a self-inventory.

Questionnaire I*

YOUR WORK ASSIGNMENT

Part A. How Good Is Your Job Module?

Pick only one question to answer among Questions 1a, 1b, and 1c and check only one block in it.

Q 1a If your work is management, in any kind of organization, please answer here, then go to Question 2.

Point Values
3 ☐ I do everything on my job, within reason, that needs to be done by one person.
2 ☐ My part of the overall task I work at is not unreasonable, but I could do a lot more.
1 ☐ My part of the overall task I work at is very small.

Q 1b If you work in manufacturing, construction, farming, etc., where something tangible is produced, please answer here, then go to Question 2.

Point Values
3 ☐ I do everything on my job that can reasonably be performed by one person. It's a good part of a whole job or product.
3 ☐ I make a whole thing, the entire thing.
2 ☐ My part of the task is small. I could do more.
1 ☐ My part of the task is very small. I could do many more things.

Q 1c If you work in a service industry, including homemaking, or if you are employed in a way that makes both Question 1a and Question 1b hard to answer, try to answer this one.

Point Values
3 ☐ I give a complete service to other people all by myself.
3 ☐ I don't give a complete service, but I give as big a part of a complete service to other people as makes good sense.
2 ☐ I participate a little in performing a service for other people, but I could do more.
1 ☐ I participate in performing a service, but not much.

*This questionnaire, as well as Questionnaire II and the Worksheet appearing later in this chapter, is distributed by Serge A. Birn Co., 1049 Bardstown Road, Louisville, KY 40704 (Tel. 502-451-6640).

Next answer Questions 2 through 5, rating your present work or assignment with regard to each of the four factors.

Q 2   How much variety is there in your assignment?

Point Values
3 ☐ A great deal.
2 ☐ Quite a bit.
1 ☐ Some; not much.
0 ☐ None worth mentioning.

Q 3   How much skill or ability is required to do the work?

Point Values
3 ☐ A great deal.
2 ☐ Quite a bit.
1 ☐ Some; not much.
0 ☐ None worth mentioning.

Q 4   Is there a lot to learn, as time passes, in your kind of assignment?

Point Values
3 ☐ A great deal.
2 ☐ Quite a bit.
1 ☐ Some; not much.
0 ☐ None worth mentioning.

Q 5   Are you responsible for a particular customer, client, or task, or is what you work at rather vague and uncertain? In other words, how clear is your responsibility?

Point Values
3 ☐ Very clear.
2 ☐ Fairly clear.
1 ☐ Not very clear.
0 ☐ Not at all clear.

Go back and add the points in front of the boxes you selected. Fifteen points (5 × 3) is the maximum.

Q 6 How many points do you have up to here?

I have _____ points thus far.

Now check the correct box below to determine the quality of your job module.

Point Values

4 ☐ Superb (15 points)
3 ☐ Good (10–14 points)
2 ☐ Poor (5–9 points)
1 ☐ Very poor (0–4 points)

But *you* get the deciding vote.

Q 7 How satisfied are you with your job module?

Point Values

3 ☐ I am completely satisfied with my job module; it is just right.
2 ☐ I am quite satisfied with my job module.
1 ☐ I am fairly well satisfied with my job module.
0 ☐ I am not satisfied with my job module.

If you checked Block 3 or Block 2, your job module is O.K., regardless of the number of points you arrived at in Question 6. However, there are other aspects of your assignment that affect your satisfaction or dissatisfaction with it. So enter the total points for the two boxes you checked in Questions 6 and 7 and then keep on going. Seven points is the limit here.

Total points for *job module* ☐

Part B. How Much Feedback Do You Get from Your Work?

Q 8 In order to do a job properly, to stay in control of it, you need to know how the job is going. How much knowledge have you as to how your job is going?

Point Values

3 ☐ I have complete knowledge, up to the minute, of how my job is going.

3 ☐ I have all the knowledge of how my job is going that I can reasonably expect.

2 ☐ I have a good but not ideal knowledge of how my job is going.

1 ☐ I have some knowledge fed to me by others about my job.

0 ☐ I have very little knowledge of how my job is going, and even that comes rather late.

0 ☐ I have almost no knowledge of how my job is going.

Q 9 How satisfied are you with your job situation so far as feedback —that is, knowledge of job results—is concerned?

Point Values

3 ☐ I am completely satisfied with the feedback I am getting.

2 ☐ I am quite satisfied with the feedback I am getting.

1 ☐ I am fairly well satisfied with the feedback I am getting.

0 ☐ I am not at all satisfied with the feedback I am getting.

Once again, add the points from the two boxes you checked in Questions 8 and 9. Six points (the limit) equals excellent feedback; 5 points, very good feedback; 4 points, fairly good feedback; 0–3 points, poor feedback.

Total points for *feedback* ☐

Part C. How Well Can You Control Your Work?

Q 10 Now rate your power to act, to control your job.

Point Values

3 ☐ I am completely in control of my work. I have all the power to act that I need if something happens.

3 ☐ I have all the power to act or control my job that I can reasonably have, but I do not have complete control.

2 ☐ I have some control over what happens on my job, but sometimes I could use a lot more.

1 ☐ I have almost no control over what happens on my job.

0 ☐ It isn't possible for anyone to have control over my kind of job.

Q 11 How satisfied are you with the amount of control or power to act that you have on your job?

Point Values

3 ☐ I am completely satisfied with the control I have.

2 ☐ I am quite satisfied with the control I have.

1 ☐ I am fairly well satisfied with the control I have.

0 ☐ I am not satisfied at all with the control I have.

Now add the points from the two boxes you checked in Questions 10 and 11. Six points (the limit) equals excellent job control; 5 points, very good control; 4 points, fairly good control; 0–3 points, poor control.

Total points for *control* ☐

Q 12 You have now finished rating your job. Add the points in the three big squares for Parts A, B, and C to get a general view of your job. Nineteen points is the limit, and 16–19 points equals an excellent job; 13–15 points, a good job; 10–12 points, a fair job; and 6–9 points, a poor job. If you rated your job only 0–5 points, either the checklist appears not to apply to all parts of it, or it is a very poor job indeed.

The *job module,* or slice of work (7-point limit)

Feedback from your work (6-point limit)

Control of the work situation (6-point limit)

Total job rating (19-point limit)

Your Job as Compared to What?

These ratings of your job are obviously subjective judgments. You made them against some standards, some hopes, some expectations of your own. Possibly you revised these standards as you went through earlier chapters of this book. And your expectations of the work situation will continue to change as you grow older and as jobs available in the marketplace change. When jobs are scarce, wise people keep a low profile. But that doesn't mean they *like* their job.

At this time, there are no national norms or figures against which to compare your score. Perhaps you would find consolation in knowing that many people rate their jobs lower than you do, or be distressed to learn that many rate their jobs higher. The figures are not available. The fact that you were able to answer the questions (if you did) indicates that you were indeed able to rate your own job against standards you hold for yourself. This is a more impressive piece of information, surely, than your standing on national norms even if they were available.

Module, Feedback, Control: A Refresher

In case you started with this part of the book because of an interest in analyzing your own job first, the following paragraphs may take the mystery out of the terms module/feedback/control. The *module* refers to the slice of work a person has. The principle is that every person should have a good slice of work, a meaningful slice, as functionally complete as makes sense. If at all possible, the person holding the job should be able to do everything needed to take care of a customer or a client. The employee working on a product should be allowed to make as much of the product as is feasible, not merely a fragment of the total. Maximize rather than minimize what any one person does, up to the point of dis-economy. If one person can't do it, build mini-groups of workers who can complete the task among themselves.

The first aspect of a good module, then, is functional completeness, and the second is a consistent situation. In a consistent job situation, employees (or a mini-group) know what part they are responsible for, which customers, which service, which part of the city. They (or the mini-group) have deadlines, perhaps weekly or monthly, and can anticipate and plan how to get the work done on time and in good order. That's part of the "fun" of a job: to plan it, organize it, and execute it.

The job of "checker" or "verifier" of someone else's work will become boring, because the checker is not producing goods or a service. Keeping the checker awake may become a job itself someday. Take the example of compiling a complete telephone directory for a city (pages 21–23). This job is a big slice of a total work flow.

Next is *feedback*. If a clerk compiled four city directories each year, then four times a year the clerk would know for certain how well he or she had performed. Why? Telephone calls from irate customers whose names are listed incorrectly will pour in, customers now receiving calls intended for the fish market will let you know about it, perhaps money must be returned to angry business people for errors in their yellow-pages advertisement. That's feedback in its best form for human motivation: "I made this directory and it is very accurate," or "I made this and I have too many errors. I must do better." It's true that the boss can motivate for the short term by hollering, refusing wage increases, and by use of other assorted pain inducers. But the enduring, motivating pain—or pleasure—comes from one's own assessment of the situation. There will be plenty of days when this complete job will cause heartaches, even if it's a good job. There will be problems and they may be all yours. But even solving a sticky problem can be "fun" of a sort. And there is always the possibility of feedback from a happy customer whose problem you solved.

Oddly enough, a job well done often elicits no praise whatsoever. No customers will telephone the clerk to say thank you for spelling their names right; customers expect that. They won't call even if you spell every name right in the entire directory. They don't know that. There are times on any job when you have got to supply your own feedback: "Well, old pal, that was a job well done." Part of the charm of a good job—or a good game—is the fact that you know when you have performed well.

As far as possible, jobs should be like interesting games, in the sense that the employee, like the bowler, golfer, bridge player, or tennis player, knows immediately the answer to the question, "How am I doing?"

If you have not been aware of the weakness of the annual performance appraisal by the boss, now you have the clue. Very likely and very often, the wrong person gives the appraisal at the wrong time. Employees should be able to appraise their own performance at the natural break points—whenever a piece of work is finished and tested. This is far more helpful than an arbitrary performance review once a year. The product should be the focus of the appraisal: how good is the product, not how good is the person. Employees get the message, without embarrassment and defensiveness, when jobs are natural modules of work with natural feedback, so that they can rate themselves. We have seen occasions when employees set higher standards and rated themselves more strictly than did the boss.

Finally, we have *control,* or the "power to act." To stay with our directory production example, if clerks know which cities are theirs, and if the irate customer's reaction can get straight through to the appropriate clerk, the module and feedback are fine. But there is another question: Does the clerk have the authority to straighten things out? Can the clerk take steps to avoid the problem in the future? If so, our three-legged stool—module/feedback/control—can stand: (1) a functionally complete and consistent module of work, (2) good feedback about how things are going, and (3) enough control to straighten things out. These are the elements of a good job for an individual. If a particular job can't be changed to meet these criteria, include it in a mini-group where the total, visible operation meets the criteria.

How Good Is Your Total Work Situation?

Questionnaire I should have given you a chance to assess the quality of your work assignment. Job quality is the central issue of this book. In the next chapter we will review steps that might be taken to improve matters. Before doing so, there are other aspects of a total job situation that you need to analyze in order for you to know where you hurt most, if you are hurting at all in your job situation. Questionnaire II will permit you to rate these other aspects.

Questionnaire II
THE TOTAL WORK SITUATION

How does your job rate with respect to—	Excellent	Good	Fair	Poor	Does Not Apply
1. Wages, salary, the money side as a whole?	——	——	——	——	——
2. Vacations and holidays?	——	——	——	——	——
3. Suitability of hours: starting, closing, length of work week?	——	——	——	——	——
4. Location and environment of the work site?	——	——	——	——	——
5. Quality and satisfactoriness of immediate supervision?	——	——	——	——	——
6. Quality of higher management?	——	——	——	——	——
7. The job done in keeping you informed about the organization as a whole?	——	——	——	——	——

8. Your rating of the people you
   work with; that is, your peers
   and the supporting staff?   —— —— —— —— ——

9. The job environment: is this a
   place where you can continue
   to learn, develop, or advance?   —— —— —— —— ——

10. The work itself that you do?
    (Bring forward your final judg-
    ment from the end of Question-
    naire I and enter it here.)   —— —— —— —— ——

Scoring instructions:

Line A: Add the number of checks
in each column.   —— —— —— —— ——

Line B: Multiply by the score value
for each column.   4   3   2   1   0

Line C: Fill in the resulting number
of points for each column.   0

Grand total of your points _____
(Add all totals noted on Line C.)

Average rating for each item _____

(Divide by 10, unless you checked fewer than 10 items. In that case drop
the unchecked items, including any that do not apply, and divide your
grand total by the number of items checked.)

First interpretation. In the first interpretation of Questionnaire II, everything is weighted equally; one item is as important as another.

*Average
Rating*

0 –0.4   This questionnaire is probably not appropriate for your job. Sorry about that.

0.5–1.4   A poor total work situation, indeed.

1.5–2.4   Fair. If you have prospects elsewhere, go now, especially if you have many remaining work years.

2.5–3.4   Don't leave this job without a good deal of thought. What does another particular job have that would justify a higher rating? Try evaluating it with this questionnaire.

3.5–4.0   What a job! Hang on to this one.

Second interpretation. In the second interpretation of Questionnaire II, all items are not equally important. How should one value these ten items, line by line? I must leave this game to you, giving you full authority to play with the 40 points involved. Rather than ten lines worth 4 points per line, it will be ten lines with a variable number of points per line. I, for one, would assign a total of 20 points to the last two lines alone. What I do with my life is as important to me now as where I do it, how I'm paid, and the suitability of hours. But I am an older person. Perhaps, for you, other lines outrank what I consider the misery of a bad job assignment.

Page 166 shows a worksheet for your use. To illustrate how it works, I have filled in two columns describing a job I recently held. In Column 1, I distributed the 40 points to indicate that the assignment is clearly most important (15 points), with a chance to learn and develop as second (5 points); that's half the points already. Higher supervision and organizational communications are not very important to me. Perhaps they are more important to you.

Worksheet

EVALUATING YOUR CURRENT JOB

	An Example		Your Own Case	
	Top Value	Job Rating	Top Value to You	Your Rating of Your Job
As previously defined:	Col 1	Col 2	Col 3	Col 4
1. Money	3	3	—	—
2. Vacations, holidays	3	3	—	—
3. Hours	3	3	—	—
4. Location	3	1	—	—
5. Immediate supervision	3	3	—	—
6. Higher supervision	1	1	—	—
7. Communications	1	1	—	—
8. Other employees	3	2	—	—
9. Chance to learn, develop or advance	5	5	—	—
10. The assignment	15	13	—	—
	—	—	—	—
Weighted job score	40	35	40	—

Average score per job factor (job score divided by 10, or the number of factors rated)	3.5	—

Scoring instructions:

First, distribute the top value of 40 points in Column 3 as you like. How important are these job factors to you, relatively? Then, in Column 4, rate your own job against the top values you have assigned to the various factors. Do not, of course, exceed the number of top-value points for any one item.

Step 1. How would you distribute your 40 points? Fill in Column 3 of the worksheet. That is your first step toward getting a sharper evaluation of your current job. Are you going to make it 4 points per item, or vary the number of points? No one else can answer for you. This is as personal as a love affair.

Step 2. The knock-down system of scoring your present job. Note my example first. I knocked down only three items from the number of points I assigned:

4. *Location.* I hated the commuting to the work location (2¹/₂ hours per day), so I knocked my rating down to 1 from my top value of 3 for that item.

8. *Other employees.* I knocked my rating down to 2 from my top value of 3, based on my appraisal of the employee's I work with.

10. *The assignment.* I knocked that down to 13 from my top value of 15. It was a staff assignment, and the tasks were often a bit vague—not quite perfect all in all, but close to it.

Now, do the same for your job. In Column 4, either write the top value you assigned in Column 3, or knock it down a bit. You can't raise it. If you knock it down to zero, that means your job fails miserably on that item. Knock it down about halfway if you want to rate your job "fair" on that item.

Step 3. Add up your points. The total cannot be more than 40. Mine comes to 35 points, for an average of 3.5. What is your average for the ten lines?

Step 4. Compare your average for the ten lines with the average you got under the first method, where the items were all worth 4 points per line. Is this sharper, weighted score more meaningful to you? Now use the information in the section "First Interpretation" to interpret your weighted score.

The average rating is only an approximation, something to ponder. There is a whole school of thought that says you cannot average factors such as these, to which I subscribe intellectually, I suppose. But you and I have got to average things like this, as a cold matter of fact. That's the way life is. Are you going to stay in this job or get out? That's the question and it involves weighting and rating various factors such as the crucial ten in the list, adding up the ratings, and making a final judgment. Using arithmetic to help you make this judgment is just a matter of convenience. If you can make a thoughtful judgment that takes all the important factors into proper account without using arithmetic, then by all means do so.

Conclusion

This chapter has stressed the *design* of the job as the culprit or the reason that the job is indeed a good one, depending on how you rated it. I hasten to acknowledge that other factors could enter into the situation, ruining a well-designed job. For example: poor training for the job, poor tools, no budget, entirely too much work for any one human being to perform, lack of sufficient personnel, weaknesses in the work chain before or after your job, or a flood of business. The purpose of the chapter, indeed of the book, is to direct your attention to job design. If the design is defective, and if you cannot, or would rather not, leave the job, can you change the situation? Let's look at some possibilities.

9

---

strategies for improving your own job

IN THE PREVIOUS CHAPTER, I suggested that you make a run for it if your current job scored extremely low. Especially if you have a number of working years ahead in your life, get out. That's more easily said than done for a person who may own a home, who has sick parents to care for, whose children need thus-and-so. There may be a hundred reasons why "make a run for it" is not helpful advice in your particular case. Nevertheless, that's the obvious and best advice up to this point, if it is suitable. Next, if your current job is not great but has possibilities, or if you can't get out of the situation, we should consider constructive strategies for building up your job. Let's examine some possibilities.

If you are merely an employee and not the boss, improving your job may seem hopeless, beyond your control. But reading this chapter and thinking about the alternatives will take only an hour of your life. That's not much of an investment of time considering the years of work remaining in most of our lives. And perhaps it will pay off by resulting in an improvement in your job situation that will make it worth holding on to not only because it's inconvenient for you to leave but because you don't want to leave it.

If you are a manager, this chapter may be helpful from two points of view. First, if your job scores low, it will suggest strategies that might help you improve it. Second, a review of these strategies may remind you of some courses to pursue that might stimulate your own subordinates and make them more productive. Consider especially any workers who have been on the job more than five years, or workers over age 40, when job malaise sometimes sets in. Are some of your people simply "running out the clock," waiting for retirement, with hopeless attitudes toward job and life?

The Objective: A Job Worth Living For

Many of us get vaguely uneasy with authors of self-help books, or even with chapters such as this. "Why does he want me to do something?" we say, restlessly. "Let bad enough alone; it's a lousy job, but all jobs are lousy."

First, all jobs are *not* equally bad. People react much more negatively to some kinds of work than to others, as was shown in Table 1 (page 4). Many people tell research workers ever so clearly that they regret having chosen their field of work, that they would change if they could start over, while others are quite happy with their choice. Although Table 1 does not include physicians, I showed it to a group of five doctors informally one evening, and asked, "Where do you think M.D.s would stand?" After complaining about seemingly endless hours, calls at night, and paper work, all five agreed that they would do it all over. Their estimate was that about 95 percent of physicians would go into medicine again.

For a happy, long life *you need to get into the right kind of work,* a job that does not "bug" you. This is not only common sense; there is medical evidence for it (see Chapter 1). Those of us who are older, who have had some very good job assignments and some very bad ones, know the difference. Many people have never had a truly good job assignment.

The purpose of this chapter is to provide you with all possible help for getting *quality* into your job if your job scored low in the last chapter. Remember, jobs at *any* level can cause employees to feel important or abandoned —jobs at any level can be jobs worth living for or not worth getting up in the morning for. I have seen executive-level scores on Questionnaire 1 that are almost at the bottom of the scale. In a project where a group of engineers were starting to redesign their jobs, one of them quietly remarked, "You know, there are a lot of great jobs in engineering; only, nobody has them." This led to, "Well, what would it take to make our jobs good jobs?" We know the generalities; now the time has arrived for getting down to individual strategies.

Strategies for Improving Your Work Situation

Although the number of strategies is limited, unfortunately, there are these five to consider before you lock yourself into a poor situation, always praying for Friday night to arrive.

GET OUT

If you are employed now, you obviously know how to go about getting a job. This time, you have more knowledge about jobs, and you have analyzed your job situation. The fastest solution is to find a job that already exists in another organization, one that comes reasonably close to meeting your needs. Remember, there are drawbacks to even the best jobs.

The tougher solution, but a dandy one if you have the courage and resources, is to start your own service or business. Then you can tailor-make the job. Millions of people do it. They go into the professions, such as medicine, dentistry, law, engineering, accountancy, and so forth, where they are either completely in charge of their own work or part of a small group, one that can control its own work flow reasonably well. Others start businesses or services with one main aim: to control what they work at themselves. If their module/control/feedback is defective, at least they are completely responsible.

A chance remark from a woman who owns her own typing and reproduction service in a small town illustrates the point. She said as she ran off copies of a letter, "This may be a stupid job, but at least it's *my* stupid job!" If your present situation scored poorly, consider changing to a better working situation, even if you have to start it yourself.

FIX IT YOURSELF

This is the hardest of the solutions to tackle; it calls for you to be the prime mover in the situation, in someone else's organization. The strategies to consider follow, and you might think of others as you read along. What can you do to improve the quality of your own job—its module, its consistency, its inclusiveness, the control of it, or the feedback from it? That's the question under review here.

If necessary, refresh your memory as to where your job seems weak, as revealed from the questionnaires in Chapter 8. Then consider these possibilities:

1. If you have anyone reporting to you or working for you, give them just as much of your job as you can, thus making time for you to expand your own *module*. Even at the risk of being unemployed, take a chance. Try fixing the flow of incoming work so that it is automatically assigned; get out of the work assignment business. Set deadlines and priorities once and for all. Then check out the other two aspects: (1) Have you given as much *control* of the work as possible to your people, or are you, for example, still reviewing, approving, and signing all the letters, reports, etc.? Do your people have power to act, or must they wait for you before they take a step? (2) Have you fixed the *feedback* loop so that they know first, and can take necessary steps without your intervention, when something goes wrong? Remember, that's the only "fun" in many jobs. Have you given your people maximum fea-

sible responsibilities, thus freeing yourself for other things? In short, would your job score better, or have an improved chance of getting better, if you gave parts of it away?

2. If you do not have people reporting to you, can you give your whole job away, nevertheless, to other people, somewhere in the organization? Can you give parts of it away, or collapse parts of your job so that you will have time to take on other aspects of the total work that truly needs to be done? Is your time filled with things you don't want to do? Would giving away parts or all of your job make a better job, a more meaningful job for the other person? This is a real possibility.

3. While you are thinking, answer this: Does this work need to be done at all? Make a tough-minded analysis of what is being done by you, and why. Use paper and pencil; diagram work flows. Speculate. Consider asking the boss that it be dropped, consolidated, or even automated. Remember, if your analysis in Chapter 8 indicated that your job is defective in some way, you have a clue to where the defect is. If your organization is a healthy, growing one, and if you collapse your job, you will become a marked person, "Hero—1st Class," one needed elsewhere, for sure. One of the sad sights of corporate life is to watch a person retire and not be replaced: The work is simply broken up and reassigned to other people. Regardless of your age, if you think your work should be broken up and given to other people, beat the company to it and enjoy a few years with a better-designed job. Make some suggestions; you won't lose.

4. If the work actually does need to be done, can you enlarge the module yourself, quietly doing more, a little bit at a time, so as not to upset routines too much? The boss might even like it. For example, one boss was accustomed to reviewing and signing all correspondence himself. One restless employee in this unit had talked several times to a certain customer by telephone, but there really needed to be a written letter of confirmation on company

stationery. The employee wrote it herself, signed it, carried it to the boss's desk and casually remarked, "I've talked to this customer twice. He wants confirmation. We have so much of this to do, do you mind if the letter goes this way?" The boss, confronted by a pile of unreviewed and unsigned letters said, "I don't see why not when it's a straightforward case. Just go ahead from now on with ones like these."

It turned out that this was a change for the better for both of them. The employee had enlarged her responsibility and the boss had more time for difficult cases. This is one example. What can you do in a similar way? Remember, I'm not suggesting that you take on the responsibility for the United Fund drive or other nonwork items. Stick with your job.

5. Even if you cannot make the prime move yourself, can you sketch alternative ways of doing that work that might be more efficient? Would a mini-group help? Can you see a way of getting your own customers, clients, turf, or task into some arrangement that would be superior to the current one, one that would give you a better piece of responsibility than you now have? Can you diagram the new arrangement, show the work flow, and prepare a presentation for someone? If so, and if you cannot be the prime mover, we are ready for the next idea.

GET HELP FROM THE BOSS

Now you are ready to talk to the boss—a most delicate moment, no doubt. All five of the "fix it yourself" strategies call for concurrence of others in the organization, especially the boss. Suppose you have decided your boss is the prime mover and that the successful redesign of your job depends upon him or her. Let your mind flow freely with questions such as the ones that follow; have a green-light session with yourself or with someone you are comfortable with.

1. How can you get the concepts of good job design across so that the boss is not threatened, does not feel you

are being unduly critical, in fact, feels the two of you are working on a common problem when you make suggestions that will result in changed work flows?

2. Can you enlist the help of your peers? How about starting bull sessions with them on the design of a good job? Should you do this before the boss is approached? Is there an educational approach that you can use that will seem helpful? What if you learn that your peers, too, rate their jobs low? Have you a common problem?

3. Can you get the boss to run a green-light session on your job and on theirs, or on the entire work flow? Might you offer to stage a green-light session exclusively aimed at the possibility of setting up a mini-group? In baiting this trap, be sure to think through and be ready to spell out your motives, for you may be viewed as an empire builder rather than as someone interested in good jobs for all. Remember the rule: "Don't steal other people's work." (If they concur in your taking it, that's not stealing.)

4. Do you dare present to the boss the alternative plans that you worked out for accomplishing work more effectively? Consider offering yourself as a guinea pig, one who might even get hurt if the plan failed or yielded no substantial gain. Recall that the fastest way to change attitudes toward a job, including your own attitude, is to change the work situation, thus first forcing behavior to change and then attitudes.

Once this redesign effort is accepted, informal "greenlighting" becomes a way of life, often occurring spontaneously. Here are two examples, one resulting in the complete elimination of a task and the other in the formation of a mini-group.

For more than 50 years, signatures on the back of a certain canceled form were inspected as the forms came back to headquarters so that any obviously fraudulent ones could be challenged. Years might go by without a challenge occurring, however. What a dull job for someone. And the flow of documents was so great that it required several people, full time, opening packets, logging them in, looking at the signatures, and stamping the back to indicate that they had looked.

Whenever there was any unusual demand for help elsewhere, these people were always tapped as an emergency squad, for their work did not affect someone else's work. This tapping became so frequent that box after box of canceled documents piled up, unopened, uninspected, and unstamped. What to do about it? Once again supervisors really needed the signature checkers elsewhere. Over coffee, the supervisors raised the question of how to get rid of this inspection/stamping job. One asked the fatal question, "Why do we do it?" No one knew for sure. "Perhaps the government requires it? The forms were valuable at one time, and fraud is a serious thing." "No," someone suggested, "the banks require that we look at the forms." "Couldn't be," countered someone else, "because the banks or a brokerage house guarantee the signature." Silence. Then: "If that's so, why do we even bother to look? We could save a thousand staff-days per year if we just let the forms go into storage."

Whereupon, one supervisor told the boss that she wanted to talk to the legal department, to find out why this ritual was necessary. "Legal" laughed and said they didn't know either, but they would find out. The result was this: Corporate bylaws required the inspection (no one else). And corporate bylaws could be changed. What did the supervisors want? They wanted to eliminate the step; merely micro-fiche the documents, as was the current practice anyhow in case of a contest, and destroy them as usual. An amendment to the bylaws was prepared. Approval by the board of directors required about 14 seconds. A terrible job was wiped out, storage space released, and supervisors had better control of the workforce. Would informal green-lighting help your job situation?

The second illustration of informal green-lighting over a conference table occurred in the Ferguson Telephone District case described briefly in Chapter 4. The supervisor of the new cathode ray tube typists was plagued by errors, absenteeism, and force loss. On one occasion the supervisors were reviewing the excellent results from the redesign of the job of the service representatives, who produced the work orders that then went to operators of the tubes. As part of the redesign of that job, the representatives' desks had been arranged in an ellipse.* One of the supervisors said, "Why can't we put the tubes right in among the service representatives so that the orders can simply be handed to the tube operators? We could form mini-groups of representatives, clerks, and tube operators. Perhaps we could give them parts of the city as their own." This was done, and it was a major contribution to the excellent performance reported in that project, but it cost that supervisor her job as boss of the tubes. The supervisors of the representatives assumed the responsibility for the tube operators also. But don't be alarmed. That supervisor, who disliked her job so much and who helped solve the problem so wisely, was immediately needed elsewhere. There is nothing wrong with being unhappy with your job, only in living with it. If the organization is not dying, you will survive.

GETTING HELP FROM THE ORGANIZATION

If you can't leave, if you can't fix the job yourself, and if the boss can't or won't fix your job, there may still be a fourth prime mover. This is the organization itself. Does it have some resources open to you? Consider these:

1. Has the organization a rotational plan? Can you get into other lines of work by formally requesting it? Rotational plans imply widening one's job knowledge and experience, not merely duplicating the current work somewhere else.

2. If you are told that you are needed for your skill at a certain kind of work, ask if it's possible to do that work

*For a diagram of the arrangement and other details, see R. N. Ford, "Job Enrichment Lessons from AT&T," *Harvard Business Review,* January–February 1973, pp. 96–106.

somewhere else. This is second-best to rotation, but at least the problems may be different, the chance to learn restored, and the new experience stimulating.

3. Can you get on task forces or committees that would challenge you more or, better yet, that might result in a change of assignment for you? This might be an important first step toward improving your situation.

4. Suggest to the people in the "right spot" of your organization that they consider a formal management training effort in the field of job design and work organization. This effort might affect your job in due time. I don't know where your company's "right spot" is; perhaps personnel, perhaps the headquarters' office of your own department. Be ready with recommendations; for example that training be done department by department, in family groups rather than in cross-sectional training sessions, where there is little chance that a redesign could occur.

5. Does your organization have an "ombudsman," someone in personnel or elsewhere who can help you get a reassignment? It is legitimate in some corporations, perhaps entirely too few, to formally place your name on a list of those who feel they could be more productive if reassigned. If there is no one formally designated for this purpose, is there anyone who might do the job of ombudsman informally? Keep this out of the "crying towel" category by being certain about why you want reassignment (see Chapter 8), by being able to state clearly what you want, and by avoiding discussion of personalities. Don't make the boss feel guilty; just get a new module of work. Consider using fairly impersonal and technical language, in fact, for it tends to be "sterilized" of emotional overtones.

URGE THE ESTABLISHMENT OF A JOB REASSIGNMENT SERVICE

If your organization has not designated someone to play the part of ombudsman, consider selling the idea within your department if not across the entire organization. This is a long-term solution to your own problem, no doubt, and one that will help your department to run more efficiently. Even if a department is so small as to make unwise the designation of a person to help with reassignments, the acceptance of the philosophy is crucial to the vitality of the organization. People have a right to be used well, not merely to be treated well. Within the limits of staying in business, the organization should have a formal way of reassigning people at their request. As a manager, you may be able to do it for your people now. If your own job is not too wonderful, and if you openly start the ball rolling for your people, you may help yourself in the long run.

Sometimes I have called this a "job repotting" service for lack of a better name. The ombudsman concept is not bad, but it implies that someone is unhappy, wants to make a complaint, and there is no one at city hall who will listen; hence the paid listener, the ombudsman, who not only will listen but will take steps. A job reassignment service goes beyond that; it may actively encourage some business for itself by announcing the establishment of the service and the rules governing its use.

Here are some considerations. Why do people at work end up in bad assignments? Perhaps the job is beyond their capabilities; they cannot demonstrate by performance that they should be promoted. Perhaps they have simply been in their job so long that they are viewed as fixtures, despite good performance. Perhaps they are happy to be underachieving or goofing off. Perhaps they were stranded, beached, because of a structural reorganization or a geographical shift. In fact, for many people, the passage of time alone may cause them to feel stranded: "I've been here too long." New laws aimed at ending one kind of stranding (women and minorities) may result in stranding other people. Nothing in this chapter will cure that problem.

To end some kinds of stranding, there is a need to sell

the organization on some variation of the following theme. Just as a house plant occasionally needs to be re-potted in fresh soil or a bigger pot if it is to thrive, so human beings seem to grow until the existing environment no longer nourishes them. There is need for a "job reassignment service"—if not a formal one, then at least an informal one—whose task is to see that people who feel pot-bound can get a job change. This is for the good of both the person and the organization. Rules such as the following need to be set up and disseminated for use as guidelines.

GROUND RULES FOR INITIATING A CHANGE IN ASSIGNMENT

1. Employees must write out a description of a job they would like to have, must be able to say why this would be a good assignment for them.
2. They cannot do this unless they have been in their current assignment at least two years (or some such minimum term).
3. They should be asked to consider submitting a job reassignment request if they have been in their current assignment ten years or more (or perhaps this should be five), but they have the right to refuse to do this. This should eliminate unthinking stagnation of assignments.
4. The boss may ask a person to initiate a request for a new assignment after two years.
5. The boss has a right to be consulted by the Reassignment Service, but cannot block a request if a change could be arranged.
6. Written requests should be forwarded to the Reassignment Service through the bosses, but bosses may delay them 30 days, as a "cooling off" period, if they wish, or as a time for them to think about changing the task assignments of employees.
7. It should not be up to the bosses to approve or disap-

prove a reassignment, but they should be allowed to change the existing job design if they wish.

CONDITIONS GOVERNING REASSIGNMENT

1. No dollar gain or loss should normally result because of the change in assignment. This is neither a bargaining tool nor a threat.
2. In due season, money changes may occur when salaries of people are being reviewed because of contracts or schedules.
3. Employees should realize that a new assignment could mean a demotion in rank, but as a rule they should not suffer financially because of this.
4. The new boss should be protected by a two-year trial period if the transfer proves to be a poor idea; the new boss should get special help in making still another reassignment for the person if the job match was a bad one.
5. The new job must never be "make work" or "busy work." It must be a real job, a real challenge.
6. Customary job bidding would have to be set aside in order to accomodate the person whose request opened the possibility for changes or created the job.
7. Interdepartmental reassignments should take priority over reassignment to one's own department, providing a whole new setting for the employee.
8. People interested in reassignment should get priority for a job over persons being considered on rotation, who may not even know they are being considered for a change.
9. If the reassignment fails to meet their expectations, employees may not ask to have their old job back nor request any other assignment for a minimum of two years.

If you truly have an unsuitable, low-scoring job as revealed by Chapter 8, you may think the above effort to get yourself repotted into a bigger job is beyond your ability. It's possible, but that will always be the case until an organization gets a mechanism started that pries people out of jobs they don't want or shouldn't have. I give you full permission to spring this repotting concept on your boss—or your organization—just as though it were your own. I will feel flattered if you do. We all will be a lot better off when any employee in an organization may say, after a reasonable length of time, "I would like a new challenge at my work." There should be no apologies necessary, just as no one need apologize in our society for attempting to be reassigned to work that pays better.

Your Personal Stance

By now, you should know definitely how well your job is suited to you. If it is inadequate and you can't leave for one that is suitable, you have considered various strategies for either improving your job or getting a reassignment within the organization. If all that fails, you have got to live with it every day, unless you are independently wealthy and can quit.

That leaves the nights and weekends. Many, many people offset poor jobs by working creatively at outside tasks. This may be right for you, too, if your regular job is not fulfilling. I'm not referring to moonlighting, which is usually a way of bolstering income. I'm thinking of men and women who work at community projects, at church or synagogue projects, or projects of professional groups or associations to which they belong. Running for office is not the same thing, either, if it is merely a way of meeting one's status needs (which we all have). But if running for office means you will then have a meaningful slice of activity, over which you will have some control and from which you will get feedback, then it can indeed help make up for a deficient regular job. Outside activities may be the final strategy to be considered by the person who is locked into a poor situation.

When I hear of men and women who are achieving well outside of working hours but who have very ordinary jobs in their big organizations, I wonder who is wrong. There are instances where they are president of the town council or school board, but not even a supervisor in their company. Surely, someone or something is wrong here; this person's talents are either being underutilized on the daily job or overutilized outside the daily job.

In your thoughts and actions about your job situation, consider taking the following stance. Accept the rightness of what you do if after carefully analyzing your job, you decide to seek a change. Don't apologize for wanting a change. Society is accepting the concept of second careers now, along with the growing national feeling that people should not be forced to retire at some arbitrary age, be it 60, 65, or 70. Know thyself and the assets and debits of your job by going through an analytic procedure such as the one described in Chapter 8. Do you want money, status, or good people to work with, or are you primarily after meaningful work? Any one of these goals is perfectly reasonable and acceptable. Or is it a balance of some sort that you seek? Enduring vague restlessness at your work is not the answer. Whining about your job is no substitute for analyzing it and trying to remedy its deficiencies. And don't worry about whether or not you fit the mold of the upwardly mobile organization man or woman. Organizations tolerate a lot of nonsense in appearance and behavior if the person runs his or her job well, if results are good, objectives are met, and good reports come back from satisfied customers. Only a dumb organization would hassle a good performer. Get yourself into such a productive situation and you can worry less about how to succeed in the organization; it will worry about you.

And this last word to the manager: All of the above goes for you and your job, of course, but you have an additional responsibility. People report to you. And most likely they have the same job needs as you—the need to feel competent and useful. Most of us, from the president of the company down to the newest employee, in the most humble job, want our days at work not to be a waste of our lives. A good assignment is the greatest gift you can give an employee.

10

---

epilog

OPEN CONCERN about the forms of work and the quality of jobs is as recent as the early 1960s. That was when job enrichment came along, concentrating on improving the quality of existing jobs. In a vague way, many felt that if people were more satisfied with their work, productivity would improve, along with quality and service. I still hold this belief based on the studies and projects in which I have participated, but many others have turned to newer solutions for problems of the workplace. Some examples: gliding time, wherein employees may come and leave at hours they prefer so long as they work a full week and are present during core hours; the four-day work week of ten hours per day, with three days off; various forms of training to raise supervisors' awareness of employees as human beings, such as sensitivity training and transactional analysis. These solutions also have the aim of helping employees to be satisfied in the workplace. All have some merit, of course; any one of these might contribute something toward the objective of a better work experience for human beings. Essentially these programs aim to adjust or adapt people to their jobs. Only one of these approaches focuses directly on the tasks that people perform, and tries to adapt jobs to people, to come up with better job designs, ones that will motivate. The other approaches try to ameliorate the pain of the workplace, without finding or eliminating the cause.

Redesigning existing jobs or designing good jobs in the first place takes time. Not too much is known as yet regarding all the parameters of a good job, but a general description can be made. Pain-killer approaches have a place. But we need to go further to learn how to build jobs that are not monotonous and soul-killing, but rather that would lead employees to say, "Since I've got to work for a living, this is where I want to work." That's not a far-fetched objective. Sooner or later, those employees may become tired of their jobs and will need to be repotted. Others may stay right on until retirement. If we can learn to build good jobs, perhaps employees will not become bored in the first two months. They may last a year, or five years, still reasonably well motivated by the job we built. I still recall a manager, now an officer of his company, who called me at the end of less than six hours on the clerical job to which he was assigned during a strike emergency. "Can you help me to get off this job, help me right now? I don't think I'll be able to last the day. It's driving me right up the wall." Yet, when there was no strike, someone performed that job all day, every day.

A "sneaky" thing has happened not only in America but throughout the industrialized world. Education levels have been rising steadily. Right now (1979) 85 percent of our young people coming into the job market ages 20 to 24 are high school graduates. By 1990, it will probably be 90 percent, when the percentage is expected to level off. That will leave only 10 percent who won't have a high school diploma. What will our job situation be at that time? People struggling only to fulfill such primary needs as food and shelter may be willing to work for anyone, at any job. To them, talk about a "meaningful" job might be nothing but "middle-class twaddle." But how about all those high school graduates? And how about half of the 20- to 24-year olds, who have gone beyond a high school education by at least one year? Interestingly enough, the proportion of high school graduates in this age group who are enrolled in college is leveling off at 33 percent, but that is a high proportion too. Do we have the correct picture in our heads as to this educational shift? We must assume that these young entrants to the job market will have high expectations of what jobs and life should be like, just as was true a few years ago when we older people came to the job market. I don't know that they are smarter; I do know that there are far more of them, actually and proportionately, than there were during World War II, by a ratio of two to one.

What will intrigue them? As far as I can see, it is jobs that have these qualities: the employees know the objectives of the organization, have a slice of a whole piece of work as their own, and have reasonable control over how they are doing it, with good knowledge of their performance and results. They, alone or as part of a mini-group, do as much toward fufilling the purpose of the organization as is possible. They or the mini-group can expand their performance as they learn, and if they perform well. "Learning" is the key word. One *learns* to be work motivated.

In a brilliant speech entitled "The Wondrous Working World of Japan," James D. Hodgson, a scholar in the field of work who had just returned from duty as U.S. Ambassador to Japan, said:

> I am suggesting that we as a nation would do well to place a stronger national commitment, first, on a flourishing economy and, second, on achieving a healthier, more positive relationship between American workers, their jobs, and their economic system, and do this through giving greater priority to treatment of our human resources in industry. I am suggesting that as a means of producing more satisfying jobs and broader employment opportunities this course holds far greater promise for the United States than does adoption of yet another parade of high-cost, fragmented governmental programs, some of which may serve somewhat to ameliorate

various national employment "problems," but which in the end do little to achieve the fundamental change needed to keep such problems from occurring in the first place.*

I agree completely. As Hodgson points out, Japanese workers—who are as highly educated as U.S. workers—come to their first job expecting to make that company their life's work. So does the company. The work ethic is deeply engrained in their culture, learned initially at home. It is reinforced at school, where acquiring a marketable skill is usually part of their educational experience.

One might be lulled into thinking that in such a society, the Japanese business person does not have to worry about the quality of jobs. People expect to work and they come to work, to produce. In my experience, no business people are more concerned than they. Japanese business people were among the first outside of the United States to inquire about the Bell System experiments. As part of an exchange of information, they showed me, in a Mitsubishi plant in Fukuyama, two ways of assembling electrical circuit-breaker boxes. The traditional assembly line, where the box moved from person to person until it was completed, was being easily surpassed in productivity by a new line where one person sat in front of a wheel of parts, assembling piece after piece until a whole circuit breaker was ready for testing. And then the person tested it, approved it, and tallied it against his or her productivity target for the day by pushing it past an automatic counter, onto a moving belt. On a small cathode screen at each workplace, these workers could press a button, see the production curve that they had plotted for the day, hour by hour, and how well they were matching that curve at the moment they pressed the button.

This was an excellent example of a complete module,

*Speech presented to the Industrial Relations Council at the University of Pennsylvania, November 1977. Available from American Enterprise Institute, Washington, D.C.

with remarkable feedback and control. If a unit did not pass the worker's inspection, he or she had to determine the cause and fix it.

The old lines were being converted to the individual positions, but a few were to be left intact for any workers who actually preferred to perform only a small act or two, repeatedly. There were some of these workers, I was told, and they were not going to be forced to work the new way. This is an idyllic example perhaps, in which home, school, and workplace all contribute to a productivity unsurpassed in the modern world. As Hodgson points out, government does not act to change this situation, either. It encourages business to be the nation's social security system.

Recognizing the merits of the Japanese way of life does not mean we should indulge in inappropriate nostalgia. Unlike Japan, America was never dedicated to a family approach to business, to joining an organization early in life, after being trained specifically for work, with the expectation of spending one's life in that organization, moving up and getting pay raises, based not on merit, but on seniority and need—"How long have you been in our family?" Competition between workers is not encouraged in Japan; consensus and group goals are the key to whatever they do. Americans can't go back to such a system; we were never there.

But we can revive the Work Ethic if we wish, not through exhortation, but through the challenge of work, by letting employees learn again that work, like other things in life, can be meaningful and satisfying. Old-fashioned time-and-motion studies, resulting in job fragmentation, did not help us. The jobs themselves must teach the Work Ethic, which is the major part of a Life Ethic, a balance between work and leisure. Good jobs have an effect on us psychologically. A psychiatrist first told me the details of a job redesign project in one of our Bell System plants that resulted in a productivity level four times as high as the previous one. Then he talked about the people in the study, and concluded, "This is one of the few examples we have of preventive psychiatry."

A final word about your job. Dr. Palmore's studies at Duke University (see Chapter 1) indicated that satisfaction with what you do can add years to your life, and common sense tells us the same thing. If you have a job that no longer meets your needs, get out or struggle to change the situation. Someone else said this first, I suppose, but I'm going to borrow it because it bears repeating here: A good job can add life to your years.

appendix

three clinical cases

THE THREE CLINICAL CASES presented here should help you test your understanding of the principles underlying the design of good work flows and jobs. (We have met these cases briefly in Chapter 2.) Read the description of the situation, decide what you would do, and then compare your answers with those of the actual managers who solved the work-flow problem. Additional copies for seminar or workshop use are available from Serge A. Birn Co., 1049 Bardstown Road, Louisville, Kentucky 40704 (Telephone: 502-451-6640).

case I

---

telephone directory compilation

JOB OBJECTIVE
To get out directories listing the telephone numbers of customers, street address, along with "yellow pages" of advertising matter for business people. This office produces 17 such books per year.

EXISTING SITUATION
Thirty-three clerks act as a team under the direction of four supervisors, getting out Directory "A" on the 1st of the month, "B" on the 18th, and so on through the year. Then the cycle is repeated. Increased activity is evidenced as the day comes for closing a book and sending it to the printer. As they pitch in to close the book, the members of the team find it difficult to get rolling and complete all orders. Turnover is high. About 2 percent of the new customer names are usually omitted from the directory. One reason for this is that service orders are in transit and are difficult to locate.

The clerks add or delete names from last year's book based on new service orders as received from another de-

Copyright © 1978, Robert N. Ford.

partment, and correct errors in last year's book, if any. The changes are reviewed and the clerks prepare copy for the printer, who proofreads the book. The accuracy measurement is based on the errors per 1,000 entries. This error rate is slowly rising, for both white and yellow pages. Yellow-pages errors are especially a problem since they result in endless calls to "Information" and often necessitate a refund to the advertiser.

All discrepancies or problems in the work of other departments or the printer are referred to the supervisor for handling. The telephone operators who use the temporary lists of monthly additions until a new book comes out have been asked to tell the directory department of any errors they notice, but this has not produced much in the way of error detection.

PROPOSALS FOR ACTION
In a "green-light" or "creative thinking" session, a number of suggestions for reshaping the clerks' jobs so as to improve the group's performance were offered by the supervisors. Twelve are shown in Exercise A; as you will notice, some of them are contradictory. About half were implemented, resulting in a dramatic improvement.

Before reading on to see what actually happened, you should complete Exercise A.

EXERCISE A

For each of the 12 actions listed below, decide whether or not it is likely to result in improvement. Put an *X* in the appropriate box in Column 1 or Column 2. Then use the boxes in Column 3 to indicate the approximate order in which you would act. This code should be helpful: ① do as soon as possible, ② do later, ③ don't do at all.

Proposed Actions	Improvement Likely		Rank Order
	Yes	No	
1. Determine the kinds of errors made and train people in how to detect them.	☐	☐	☐
2. Add more supervisors to the unit, at least until results improve.	☐	☐	☐
3. Arrange for additional checks at appropriate points along the process route.	☐	☐	☐
4. Add variety to the work by letting clerks work on as many different cities as possible.	☐	☐	☐
5. Determine which clerks have good job knowledge already.	☐	☐	☐
6. Give some clerks only one book to work on until it is completed.	☐	☐	☐
7. Permit each clerk to keep his or her own file of orders handled.	☐	☐	☐
8. Have coordination meetings to keep abreast of "where we are."	☐	☐	☐
9. Give the clerks the monthly and yearly due dates of book closings.	☐	☐	☐
10. Give some clerks only a piece of a large book to work on.	☐	☐	☐
11. Increase the number of clerks reporting to each supervisor.	☐	☐	☐
12. Permit clerks to contact directly other groups or agencies involved in directory compilation.	☐	☐	☐

WHAT ACTUALLY HAPPENED

Items 5, 6, 10, 7, 9, and 12 were actually implemented in that order. It was found that the clerks did not feel they had a full measure of responsibility for the directories they were producing. Each did only a fraction of the work on all books. Once clerks of proven competence were given a complete piece of work (a whole book, two or more books, or, in the case of a very large book, an alphabetical segment), they began to feel accountable for every entry that went into or out of "their" directory. Accuracy improved to the point where two of the four verifications that had previously been carried out were eliminated. The file clerks, no longer needed, were reassigned elsewhere. Proportionately, the number of supervisors dropped even more.

About 2 percent of new customers had previously been omitted from each book, at closing, because of uncompleted processing. Now only one-quarter of 1 percent actually were still out at closing. This meant that instead of 4,000 customers, only 900 were omitted.

Clerks who now "own" a book really need their own files, they say. Turnover is dropping.

CONTINUING THE MOTIVATIONAL THRUST

The motivational responsibility of a manager never ends with a new job design. Work changes, shortages occur, demand shifts unexpectedly. Also, new people enter the work unit and older ones leave, thus changing experience levels. And, in addition to the never-ending special cases, supervisors may suggest further changes in job design affecting everybody in the unit. Exercise B is drawn from 11 actual suggestions that arose from the directory-compilation case.

EXERCISE B

Some possible further motivators are listed here. First, decide in each case which motivational route is being proposed. Is the suggestion an attempt to motivate through changing the work itself (*internal* motivation), or is it essentially an attempt to raise motivational levels through changes in the rewards of work (*external* motivation)? Put an *X* in the appropriate column.

Second, would you recommend following the suggestion or not? *Yes* or *No*? What are the pros and cons, especially in view of potential costs? Some items might operate as motivators either way, depending on the view you take, thus making them especially worthy of consideration.

Some possible further motivators	Kind of Motivation		Would You Recommend?	
	Internal	External	Yes	No
1. Put clerk's name in book.				
2. Put clerk's picture in book.				
3. Let employee design cover.				
4. Place clerks in a higher job grade with a new title but no added salary.				
5. Grant the higher salary but do not change either wage grade or title.				
6. Let employees set their own hours of starting and leaving, provided they work a full day.				
7. Let employees form work teams if they wish, even though one clerk could produce a book alone.				
8. Encourage formation of bowling teams or other out-of-hours activities.				
9. Let clerks talk to printer about directory problems.				
10. Let clerks set deadlines for book closing and sale of advertising.				
11. Let clerk involved talk directly to person who sold yellow-pages advertisement.				

Answers for Exercise B

Kind of Motivation	Would You Recommend?	Pros and Cons
1. External	Yes	O.K. to offer, but in the United States, women especially are likely to refuse the honor for fear of nuisance calls at night.
2. External	Yes	Same as above; expect "no sale."
3. Internal	No	The cover is part of the book, but artwork and different print runs are costly. O.K. to settle for a few choices.
4. External	Yes	"Dry raises" are not much fun, but if that were all I could do, I'd do it.
5. External	Yes	Perhaps Items 4 and 5 could be combined. Union contracts, bargaining, and economic issues will decide.
6. Both	Yes	Internal in that "gliding time" might permit workers to have better access to computers, Xerox, etc., and result in better day-long office coverage and customer service. External in that hours will better fit personal needs (home, children, commuting).
7. Both	Yes	Minigroups of mutually supporting workers may out-produce individual workers while providing a place for new employees to learn and advance more easily, providing better coverage in time of illness, high workloads, etc. In addition, minigroups meet the external need for friendly human association.
8. External	No	The cost-effectiveness of such parternalistic programs is questionable.
9. Internal	Yes	For many reasons, shorter lines of communication usually win.
10. Internal	Yes	Experience shows that employees in this situation often set harder deadlines than the bosses might.
11. Internal	Yes	Same as No. 9.

case II

---

typewriter assembly line

JOB OBJECTIVE

When a typewriter assembly or subassembly reaches your position, note the model, add the correct parts from your bin or bins, and push the machine onward. Length of work cycle: 3 minutes maximum. More than 2,000 parts are involved.

EXISTING SITUATION

This IBM plant in Amsterdam makes and ships typewriters to 80 countries in Europe and Asia: 18 basic models, 25 specials. The plant opened in 1961; it is quite modern and well located. By 1969, the plant had two production lines, each more than 300 meters (984 feet) long, and a total of 1,600 people. In early 1970, a sales projection shows that the plant must double again by 1973 to meet growing demands. Management is sure it cannot make that target by merely adding two more long, continuous lines. National headquarters shares the view; the plant may have to be moved. Similar work is done in Kentucky, Toronto, and Texas.

Copright © 1978, Robert N. Ford.

The competition for labor is fierce, and employees who quit say that the assembly line is a place for idiots or robots. Force loss (turnover) is at an unbearable rate of 30 percent per annum. Daily absence averages 6 percent. Before and after weekends and holidays, the production lines often stop, or accordion-like waves occur because of absenteeism and the presence of untrained persons trying to fill in. Workers come from many nations; there are 12 different languages spoken by employees in the plant (Spanish, Turkish, Italian, Yugoslav, etc.). By Dutch law, 4 percent of all workers must be hired from among the nation's handicapped. The plant is essentially not unionized. By law, also, there exists a works council upon which employees sit by election.

As a typewriter moves along the straight line, which is longer than a football field, it moves through five departments, the last two being adjustment and testing, where many typewriters are turned back. Current error rate, 2.7 per machine. Labor represents 90 percent of the cost of a machine, and 12 percent of the 90 percent is the cost of repairing errors, usually at overtime pay rates. Parts are made elsewhere in the plant or overseas.

The three top managers agree that they will lose the plant if they try to meet rising demands by doing more of the same. In Holland as in the United States, virtually all job applicants at such plants are high school graduates, many with even more education than that.

PROPOSALS FOR ACTION

The three top managers came up with a list of "green-light" suggestions similar to those in Exercise A. Some of them were implemented. As a result, production improved so much that plants in Kentucky and Ontario took steps of the same kind.

Before reading on, complete Exercise A. Then compare your answers to what was actually done.

EXERCISE A

For each of the 16 actions listed below, decide whether or not it is likely to result in improvement. Put an X in the appropriate box in Column 1 or Column 2. Then use the boxes in Column 3 to indicate the approximate order in which you would act, with a value of 1 for "do as soon as possible," 2, "do later," and 3, "don't do at all."

	Improvement Likely		Rank
Proposed Actions	**Yes**	**No**	**Order**
1. Continue with two production lines but get rid of all foreign language groups except one in each of the two long lines.	☐	☐	☐
2. Set as an objective the elimination of half the foreign groups within one year.	☐	☐	☐
3. Let workers on the lines schedule their breaks for rest and lunch when they desire.	☐	☐	☐
4. Let workers schedule starting hours also.	☐	☐	☐
5. Break the two long lines into eight or ten short ones with far fewer workers per line.	☐	☐	☐
6. Expect and train workers to do far more, perhaps by lengthening the work cycle to as much as ten minutes.	☐	☐	☐
7. Shorten the work cycle to perhaps one minute and train harder at skill and accuracy.	☐	☐	☐
8. Let each person make a complete typewriter, which he or she tests.	☐	☐	☐
9. Make the production line U-shaped or M-shaped, with workers inside so they can consult one another about problems and see the final product.	☐	☐	☐
10. Let workers be responsible for their own parts inventory and also for the acceptability of parts or subassemblies.	☐	☐	☐
11. Encourage language groups to work together and help each other on numerous shorter production lines.	☐	☐	☐
12. Introduce a wage incentive system.	☐	☐	☐
13. Let the two long lines remain, but start up new, shorter lines with longer work cycles for better workers to meet higher product demand.	☐	☐	☐
14. Abandon the five-department approach. Set up shorter lines responsible for all five steps, including testing.	☐	☐	☐

15. Avoid setting up shorter lines since that would cause the unnecessary expense of duplicate tooling.   □   □   □

16. Get handicapped workers off the lines into other kinds of work in the plant.   □   □   □

WHAT ACTUALLY HAPPENED

The plant managers asked their supervisors to implement these items: 13, 14, 9, and 6 (first priority) and 10, 11, 3, 4, and 5 (second priority). Item 5 was to provide the final outcome, but it had to be approached gradually. Supervisors fought the plan initially; they felt left out of the planning. They believed that shorter work cycles and harder efforts by the training department were the likeliest solutions to their problems.

The changeover caused production to dip for one month only, whereas management had expected a three-month dip. With the 1971 production level as 100 percent, that for 1972 rose to 135 percent and that for 1973 to 146 percent, at which time the plants in North America moved to either M-shaped or U-shaped lines, in which the final product is always in view. This permits quick changes and adjustments in procedure if testing reveals that trouble is starting. Language groups tend to work together, as do the handicapped.

There is much greater production flexibility with the shorter lines. For example, starting up production of a new kind of machine is much easier.

The parts inventory is much smaller since the employees took responsibility for keeping only enough parts on hand for the work ahead. This saved floor space and greatly reduced product handling. Each group has been given its own hand truck, which the members use both to get parts and to take the final product away. They have decorated their trucks, and the fact that they refuse to lend them to one another does not disturb management a bit.

Force loss, or turnover, dropped 20 percent in the first year and a further 10 percent during the second year. Not only does this reflect savings for the training department, but it means a more experienced workforce and a more nearly error-free product. Absenteeism has dropped.

The employees requested "gliding time" for their "cocoa breaks" and also for the lunch period. This has resulted in much better usage of the lunch and restroom facilities. Also, if a production problem arises, the group concerned can take its break until the problem is solved. Gliding time has been extended to the starting and therefore the quitting hour, resulting in fewer traffic jams in the parking lot. When overtime becomes necessary for a line, scheduling is much less complicated; fewer people need to be in the plant.

This IBM plant calls its groups "minilines." Some "microlines" have been established within the minilines to perform certain subassembly work, this in response to a suggestion made by workers.

The error rate per machine is virtually zero as product after product leaves the miniline. There is no formal inspection along the line now; it merely takes place at the end. The number of indirect-cost workers is dropping proportionally, and the relative size of the supervisory force is likewise falling.

case III

the long-distance frameman's job

JOB OBJECTIVES
Craftsmen in Group I: To make the necessary cross-connections on the main frame of a telephone central office when a customer requires a new circuit or, if additional circuits are required, between offices of telephone companies. Circuits may carry voice, data, TV signals, etc. Approximately 40 people usually work in groups of three, two of whom do the soldering while the "whip," the third person, runs the wires from one location to the other. At least some workers are present night and day, year-round. This is the problem group.

Craftsmen in Group II: To write up the equipment cross-connection cards, detailing the equipment to be changed or added and the circuits to be connected on the basis of the circuit order and engineering drawings. This work is done by other craftsmen reporting to other managers. Still other workers in Group II change the equipment while Group I does the wiring. Then people in Group II test the circuit for continuity and quality, while still others turn up the circuit and inform the customer or the local company of its readiness.

Copyright © 1978, Robert N. Ford.

EXISTING SITUATION

The workers in Group I are unofficially limiting production to 21 "jumpers" (cross-connections) per day per person. The bosses know this. They hear the workers say quietly, "The phantom walked," which means, "That's all for today." Formal grievances average one per week; a tense union situation exists. Workers call themselves "frame apes," claiming that "anyone can learn the job in a week. Grab a card, solder the jumper connections indicated, mark it completed, and get another card. It doesn't take any intelligence."

The frame-error level on the new circuits is unacceptably high. When the person from Group II who is doing the testing has any difficulty, he or she informs the Group II supervisor, who relays the information to the supervisor in Group I. The framemen then on duty repair the circuit. Finding out who actually made the error is costly and likely to cause still more trouble. Workers blame other workers for splashing solder and the like. To avoid this confrontation, errors are simply corrected and a chart showing the number of errors per day is posted on a bulletin board. The curve on this chart is rising.

In addition, an easy-to-read chart showing the percentage of work completed on time is posted daily. The percentage is steadily falling, circuits not completed on time have reached the 50 percent level. And circuits that don't exist (or don't work) earn no revenue. They are an expensive proposition.

Actually, some of the many errors are traceable to errors in the order write-up for the circuit as it comes from Group II. The workers in both groups tend to be older persons; the average age is 46. And all jobs pay alike when workers are earning top rates because of their long years of service.

PROPOSALS FOR ACTION

The higher-level boss responsible for the area insists that something be done. The first item in the "green-light" list in Exercise A is his. Other proposals have come from supervisors. Some of them have resulted in remarkably improved performance on the part of the workers.

Before reading on, do Exercise A.

EXERCISE A

For each of the 16 actions listed below, decide whether or not it is likely to result in improvement. Put an *X* in the appropriate box in Column 1 or Column 2. Then use the boxes in Column 3 to indicate the approximate order in which you would act, with a value of 1 for "do as soon as possible," 2, "do later," and 3, "don't do at all."

	Improvement Likely		Rank Order
	Yes	No	
1. Divide the workers into groups and have them specialize in only one kind of circuit work.	☐	☐	☐
2. Train everyone to know and avoid the causes of errors.	☐	☐	☐
3. Let the framemen (Group I) make the equipment changes prior to soldering.	☐	☐	☐
4. Keep the workers on the circuit until a tester from Group II releases them.	☐	☐	☐
5. Let the "whip," after the necessary training, be responsible for testing as well as running the wires.	☐	☐	☐
6. Let groups of three decide themselves who shall organize the day's work and be the whip, once they can test circuits.	☐	☐	☐
7. Let the whip authorize overtime.	☐	☐	☐
8. Let groups, rather than the supervisor, orient new employees or visitors.	☐	☐	☐
9. Let testers from Group II meet with framemen one hour each week to review errors and avoidance procedures.	☐	☐	☐
10. Let whips appoint their own replacements if they must be absent.	☐	☐	☐

11. Let team members contact supervisors in other locations (or customers) directly about the work being performed.   ☐   ☐   ☐

12. Let a team member represent a group or several groups at information meetings about the United Fund, vacation plans, and other out-of-hours activities.   ☐   ☐   ☐

13. Let a team member represent a frame group at interoffice, intra-office, and departmental meetings whenever possible when work problems or changes arise.   ☐   ☐   ☐

14. Let a team determine job priority once it has been given a due date.   ☐   ☐   ☐

15. Stop team members from negotiating directly with supervisors of other groups when the workload demands extra people, so that the workers will stick to their own jobs.   ☐   ☐   ☐

16. Train the teams and plan their membership so that each can do all the jobs done by various people in Groups I and II.   ☐   ☐   ☐

WHAT ACTUALLY HAPPENED

The supervisors actually implemented 9 of the 16 items: 5, 3, 6, 14, and 13 (first priority) and 11, 10, 8, and 16 (second priority). Item 16 was the long-run solution to the whole problem. It had to be approached in stages.

Results were dramatically good as compared with those previously recorded. However, reasonably comparable results were observed for a control group in another building, which indicates that further improvement should be possible. Among the improvements resulting from the project were the following:

1. The number of work units per person rose. Remarks about the "phantom" and the restriction of output to 21 "jumpers" gradually disappeared.

2. Circuits completed on time rose from 50 percent almost to the 100 percent level.

3. Frame errors, previously one of the most serious problems, fell almost to zero once the team knew how to test a completed circuit.

4. Regarding the tender issue of grievances, the final report reads: "Perhaps one of the most meaningful obser-

vations is the fact that no formal grievances were received from this group during the entire period of this study. Prior to the project, grievances averaged about one each week." Incidents were handled on a "deskside" basis.

5. Employees who were not fully trained pressured supervisors to give them the opportunity to qualify for greater responsibility. No money was involved.

6. Framemen no longer wait for assignments at the beginning of a tour. "They come in, select the circuit that they want to work on, and proceed to complete the job."

7. "Employees not in the study group are requesting to be assigned to that group."

8. "There is great satisfaction in having the circuit meet the tests on the first attempt. Previously the testers from Group II didn't care a bit if the circuit succeeded or failed; they had not done the work. And the members who had done it were off somewhere else or had gone home for the day. The circuit tester's job was obviously made more meaningful, as well as the job of the wireman." Team members enjoy calling a customer to say that the circuit is ready.

9. Unstated in the formal report, but equally important, is the reaction of the managers. Remarks like these were common: "At last I have time to manage." "The boss need no longer try to be the fastest soldering gun in the West— that's the solderman's job." "I don't care what anyone else does when this study period is over. *We* are going to continue working this way."

10. Under this way of working, finally, the number of workers per supervisor rose as new people were added. This obviously made possible an important saving in the cost of supervision.

CONTINUING THE MOTIVATIONAL THRUST

A number of further suggestions arose in the case of the long-distance frameman's job, aimed at maintaining the improved motivational level resulting from the initial job redesign effort. Exercise B is drawn from these suggestions.

EXERCISE B

Some possible further motivators are listed here. First, decide in each case which motivational route is being proposed. Is the suggestion an attempt to motivate through changing the work itself (*internal* motivation), or is it essentially an attempt to raise motivational levels through changes in the rewards of work (*external* motivation)? Put an X in the appropriate column).

Second, would you recommend following the suggestion or not? *Yes* or *No*? What are the pros and cons, especially in view of potential costs? Some items might operate as motivators either way, depending on the view you take, thus making them especially worthy of consideration.

Some Possible Further Motivators	Kind of Motivation		Would You Recommend?	
	Internal	External	Yes	No
1. Ask workers to raise their productivity to 22 jumpers, then 23, etc., until a quota of 25 is reached.				
2. Mount a campaign to end use of the offensive term "frame ape."				
3. Have someone make an organizational chart, with pictures of the team members, for posting on the bulletin board.				
4. The same idea—but prepare the chart in booklet form to be sent to customers or clients.				
5. Increase the wages of the team members if they improve their productivity.				
6. Let workers set their own hours of starting and leaving, provided they work a full shift.				
7. Let workers decide, if they wish, who shall be on their team.				
8. Let repeat orders from the same customer or client go to the same team whenever possible.				
9. Let workers invite customers to see the frame room. Show them how the work of providing private lines is done.				

ANSWERS FOR EXERCISE B

Kind of Motivation	Would You Recommend?	Some Pros and Cons
1. External	No	They are not offering to increase their productivity. One hopes they will reach these levels, or even higher ones, but this will seem like typical managerial goal setting.
2. External	No	This is your campaign, not theirs. When they are no longer merely "frame apes" but are doing many jobs, the term may disappear.
3. External	No	A chart like this may be interesting for a while but is largely functionless. At best it gratifies people's egos.
4. Both	Yes	May have motivational value if cost permits. It is ego-gratifying and may help customers and clients to determine who can clear up problems quickly.
5. External	No	Not feasible in this particular national bargaining situation. When, and if, the job is more productive, bargaining will take care of it.
6. Both	Yes	If possible. "Gliding time" might permit teams to start and stop jobs more conveniently for customers and, at the same time, meet home and personal needs more fully. But, in this three-shift, 24-hours-a-day situation, the motivational value is limited.
7. Both	Yes	If team members are chosen for their skill and competence, there may be *internal* motivation—the desire to see work well done. If they are chosen purely for companionship, the result will be *external* motivation, which is not necessarily bad.
8. Internal	Yes	Extremely effective. Actually done in another location.
9. Internal	Yes	There are elements of both internal and external motivation here, as in many of the previous suggestions, but the effect is to heighten the drive toward work.

bibliography

Bartlett, L E., *New Work/New Life.* New York: Harper & Row, 1976.

Bugg, R., *Job Power.* New York: Pyramid, 1976.

Cass, E. L., and F. G. Zimmer, *Man and Work in Society.* New York: Van Nostrand Reinhold, 1975.

Cooper, R., *Job Motivation and Job Design.* London: Institute for Personnel Management, 1974.

Davis, L. E., and J. C. Taylor (eds.), *Design of Jobs.* London: Penguin, 1972.

Foulkes, F. K., *Creating More Meaningful Jobs.* New York: AMACOM, 1969.

Gooding, J., *Job Revolution.* New York: Walker, 1972.

Hackman, J. R., and J. L. Suttle (eds.), *Improving Life at Work.* Santa Monica, Cal.: Goodyear, 1977.

Herzberg, F., B. Mausner, and B. Snyderman, *Motivation to Work.* New York: Wiley, 1959.

Herzberg, F., *Work and the Nature of Man.* Cleveland, Ohio: World, 1966.

Horabin, I., *Toward Greater Employee Productivity.* Summit Point, W. Va., 1971.

Huizinga, G., *Maslow's Need Hierarchy in the Work Situation.* Groningen, Netherlands: Wolters-Noordhoff, 1970.

Jenkins, D., *Job Power.* New York: Doubleday, 1973.

Kobayashi, S., *Creative Management.* New York: AMACOM, 1970.

Levitan, S. A., and W. B. Johnston, *Work Is Here to Stay, Alas.* Salt Lake City: Olympus, 1973.

Maher, J. (ed.), *New Perspectives in Job Enrichment*. New York: Van Nostrand Reinhold, 1971.

McLean, A. (ed.), *Mental Health and Work Organizations*. Chicago: Rand McNally, 1970.

Myers, M. Scott, *Every Employee a Manager*. New York: McGraw-Hill, 1970.

———, *Managing Without Unions*. Reading, Mass.: Addison-Wesley, 1976.

Palmore, E., and F. C. Jeffers, *Prediction of Life Span*. Lexington, Mass.: Heath, 1971.

Rosow, J. M. (ed.), *Worker and the Job*. Englewood Cliffs, N.J.: Prentice-Hall, 1974.

Schrank, R., *Ten Thousand Working Days*. Cambridge, Mass.: MIT Press, 1978.

Sheppard, H. L., and N. Q. Herrick, *Where Have All the Robots Gone? Worker Dissatisfaction in the Seventies*. New York: The Free Press, 1972.

Swedish Employers' Confederation, *Autonomous Groups and Payment by Results*. Stockholm, 1973.

———, *Saab-Scania Report*. Stockholm, 1973.

———, *Job Reform in Sweden*. Stockholm, 1975.

———, *Matfors Report*. Stockholm, 1975.

———, *Orrefors Report*. Stockholm, 1975.

———, *Volvo Report*. Stockholm, 1975.

Tausky, C., *Work Organizations*. Itasca, Illinois: Peacock, 1970.

Terkel, S., *Working*. New York: Pantheon, 1972.

U.S. Department of Health, Education, and Welfare, *Work in America: Report of a Special Task Force to the Secretary of Health, Education, and Welfare*. Cambridge, Mass.: MIT Press, 1973.

U.S. Senate, *Worker Alienation, 1972* (Hearings before the Committee on Labor and Public Welfare, U.S. Senate, 92nd Congress, S3916, July 25–26, 1972). Washington, D.C.: U.S. Government Printing Office, 1972.

Walters, R. W., *Job Enrichment for Results*. Reading, Mass.: Addison-Wesley, 1975.

Whitehill, A. M., Jr., and S. I. Takezawa, *The Other Worker*. Honolulu: East-West Center Press, 1968.

Yorks, L., *Radical Approach to Job Enrichment*. New York: AMACOM, 1976.

index

Work Is Here to Stay, Alas
(Levitan and Johnston), 7,
64
work organization, *see* job
design
workweek, *xiii–xiv,* 78–79, 82,
185

youth
job expectations of,
education and, 7–10, 66,
186–187
restructuring jobs for,
66
work motivation for, 52, 65